ANCIENT ROME

Christoph Höcker

BARRON'S

Cover photos from top to bottom and left to right:
The masks of comedy and tragedy, Roman mosaic from Pompeii. Rome, Capitoline Museum /
Roman Colosseum. Copper engraving, Archive for Art and History (AKG), Berlin / Etruscan
Amphora. Berlin, Pergamon Museum (Photo: AKG, Berlin, Erich Lessing) / Dyptichon of
Arcobines. Paris, Cluny Museum (Photo: Hamburg, Archaeological Institute) / The Capitoline
Wolfe. Rome, Copiloting Museum, Conservators Palace (Photo: AKG, Berlin, Erich Lessing) /
Roman gold armband. Vienna, Art History Museum (Photo: AKG, Berlin, Erich Lessing) / Bust of
Gaius Julius Caesar. Berlin, Ancient Collection (Photo: bpk) / *Antefix* with head of a maenid.
Rome, Etruscan sculpture. Villa Giulia National Museum (Photo: AKG, Berlin) / Laocoon group.
Plaster cast. Vatican Museums (Photo: AKG, Berlin) / Hannibal in Capua. Reconstruction.
© P. Conolly, Spalding / Asterix and Maestria. Paris, © 1997, Les Editions Albert René
Back cover photos from top to bottom:
Gold coin with emperor's image, reign of Constantine. (Photo: AKG, Berlin) / Roman relief of
painted terra cotta. Augustan. Rome, Antiquario Palatino (Photo: AKG, Berlin, Werner Froman)
/ Theodor Mommsen. Photograph, 19th century. (Photo: AKG, Berlin)
Frontispiece:
Rome—ancient and modern: perplexed visitor standing in the courtyard of the Conservators
Palace in front of the ruins of a monumental statue of Constantine the Great. (Photo: Martin
Thomas)

American text version by: Editorial Office Sulzer-Reichel, Overath, Germany
Translated by: Sally Schreiber, Friedrichshafen, Germany
Edited by: Bessie Blum, Cambridge, Mass.

First edition for the United States and Canada
published by Barron's Educational Series, Inc., 1997.

First published in the Federal Republic of Germany in 1997 by
DuMont Buchverlag GmbH und Co. Kommanditgesellschaft, Köln.

All inquiries should be addressed to:
Barron's Educational Series, Inc.
250 Wireless Boulevard
Hauppauge, New York 11788

Library of Congress Catalog Card No. 97-71964

ISBN 0-7641-0244-3

Printed in Italy by Editoriale Libraria

Contents

Preface   7
The Cultural Environment: Greeks, Etruscans, Italics   8
The indigenous and the immigrant: Cultures and cultural conflicts on the Apennine
peninsula/The Etruscans: Religion, state, economy, society/The Etruscan script/
Etruscan tombs as a mirror of life/The Tuscan-Roman temple
The Roman Religion   20
From Romulus to Caesar: The Roman Republic   24
The founding of Rome and the time of the kings/From village to state: Confedera-
tions, wars, and the Republic as a model of sovereignty/Rome between the aristo-
cracy and the people: Social crises and their significance for the republican state
The Roman Navy   32 *c.1*
From a confederation of cities to dominance: Politics and the military/City and
country, freedmen and slaves: The republican economy and its crises
Imperial Portraiture   42
State and Society: The View from the Upper Class   44
Augustus—or republic lost/The aristocracy's economic base: Country villas, town
houses, and free time/Politics, mythos, and art: Artistic media as the organ of
ideology
More than Money: Roman Coins   50
Splendor and luxury of the Roman upper classes/Art thieves and copyists: Greek art
in a new context/Culture versus nature: A universal contradiction as social motto
Roman Classicism   62
Daily Life in Roman Cities   64
Big cities and slums: In the shadow of ancient architecture/Roman recreation
The Roman House   68
Urban society
The Family   74
Craft, trade, and processing raw materials: The business and labor world
between class organization and slavery/The pageantry of the "little man":
The self-dramatization of the middle class/Of poverty and banditry
Wall Paintings: The Four Pompeian Styles   82
Medicine and pharmacology

Rome and Its Provinces 88

The creation and administration of the empire/The *limes* and its *castella*/
The "urbanization" of the military camps: The creation of new provincial centers

Roman Building Technology 96

Commercial traffic in the Roman empire/Surveying: Engineering as
domination

Water Conduits, Streets, and Bridges 102

Crisis and Downfall 104

The crisis of the Roman empire in the 3rd century AD/Searching for solutions:
The empire as an object of reform

The Roman Army 108

The Late Antiquity: Modern expression or historical epoch?/*Munera* and urban
flight: The last antique domain as image of the world/Rome and the Christians

The Catacombs 118

The heirs of ancient Rome: Byzantium, Arab world, Langobardic-western culture

Rome's Afterlife in the Medieval and Modern Worlds 124

Rome as idea: Roman concepts of law and state in the postclassical world/
Ancient artifacts

Roman Remains in the Vicissitudes of Time 130

Lasting beauty and elemental greatness: Ancient Rome and the cult of ruins/
Rome as utopia: The American and the French Revolutions

Triumphal Arches, City Gates, Villas:
Motifs in Renaissance Architecture and Drawing 138

Ancient Rome and the Wilhelmine idea of the "German"/
The ancient, the modern, and dictatorship: The role of Roman antiquity in
Fascism and Nazism

Decadence and Imitation: How a Culture Acquires an Image 156

Ancient Rome and Modern Studies 158

The transmission of the ancient Roman world/The excavation of a culture: The discoveries
of Pompeii and Herculaneum/Between progress and fantasy: Experimental archaeology/
In lieu of conclusion: Ancient Rome from the perspective of contemporary ancient studies

Glossary 172
Historical Overview—A Short Survey of the History of Ancient Rome 174
The Roman Emperors 177
Museums and Collections of Roman Art and Cultural History;
    Important Archaeological Excavations 177
Selected Bibliography 181
Index of Places 184
Index of Names 187
Picture Credits 192

Preface

Prejudices about ancient Rome are common—that ancient Rome was only a marginal epoch, that Roman culture was an inferior appendage to the high culture of Greece characterized by artistic imitation, political despotism, social decay, moral decadence, and religious confusion, and demonstrating merely technological initiative. Such beliefs are scarcely worth repeating or elaboration. This volume, rather, seeks to challenge such traditional clichés in the light of revised modern perceptions, and also to consider the reasons behind such possibly misplaced value judgments and the mechanism by which they have grown and survived. The negative judgment of Rome is a viewpoint that had even in ancient times fostered a one-sided understanding of Roman culture that persists today in novels, films, and comics—as well as in classes in ancient languages.

To capture the wealth of material from this thousand-year period of world and cultural history may seem daunting to both author and reader. Still, it is possible within a limited scope to assemble a multifaceted kaleidoscopic portrait of ancient Rome—from the beginnings of the ethnically diverse Apennine peninsula around 600 BC to the transfiguration of tyrannical monarchy into a "Golden Age" and the gradual disintegration into a new cultural subsystem in the Late Antiquity. Throughout, ancient Rome proved itself on the whole dynamic—a world culture that could absorb the most distinct regional cultures with their own native traditions into a new whole.

This chronological explanation of the history of ancient Rome is enhanced by interrelated tangential glimpses into certain aspects of Roman life, to bring the era to life more fully for the reader. This crash course offers a number of excursions into archeological findings and excavations, architecture and artwork, tombs, literature and inscriptions, as well as social and regional life. Thus, on the one hand, the book presents a single connected narrative, while on the other hand, individual chapters serve as self-contained units.

This book diverges from common practice by declining to present the Roman epoch as a clearly defined period of ancient history, with a clear beginning and end, wholly cut off from the here and now. Instead, this volume attempts to address all aspects of Roman antiquity, especially regarding the "survivors" of the period—not only the Latin Middle Ages, the Byzantine East, and the Islamic Orient, but also the Renaissance, the French Revolution, the American Revolution, and fascist Italy—for all of which antique Rome has been a model for ideas of state, architecture, and art. This history of the influence of Rome on subsequent ages and cultures receives as much attention as the narrative account provided by research and oral tradition, whose many forms and contradictory movements document how closely our views of the past are anchored in who we ourselves are.

Christoph Höcker

1000 – 500 BC

After ca. 925 Villanova culture thrives as predecessor of the Etruscans

ca. 814 Carthage founded

760–653 25th dynasty in Egypt: beginning of the Late Period

after 754 Greek colonization of the Apennine peninsula

754 *Pithekusai* on the island of Ischia

ca. 750 Cumae, Italy's earliest Greek colony

ca. 740 Greek colonies: Rhegium (Reggio/Calabria), Croton, and Sybaris

ca. 700 Tarentum. Sparta conquers Messenia; formation of the Spartan state (Great Rhetra)

ca. 690 Caulonia and Metapontum

ca. 650 Locris. Revolt of the Helots in Messenia against Sparta

ca. 650–600 Poseidonia (Paestum)

ca. 624 Draco gives Athens its first laws

612 Downfall of Nineveh, end of the Assyrian kingdom

600–500 Pandosia, Pyxus, Laos, Temesa, Terina, Scylletium, Hipponion, Medma (exact founding dates unknown)

594–593 Solon becomes lawgiver in Athens

547 Cyrus conquers the Lydian kingdom of Croesus

ca. 540 Elea (Velia)

539 Cyrus conquers Babylon; beginning of the Achmeaid domination of Mesopotamia and Asia Minor

ca. 480 Neapolis (Naples)

444–443 Thurioi

433–432 Heraclea in Siris

The indigenous and the immigrant: Cultures and cultural conflicts on the Apennine peninsula

In order to grasp the complex entity that is Roman antiquity and to understand its idiosyncratic details, we must first look back to the cultural setting on the Italian peninsula in the first half of the 1st millennium BC. The long and narrow Apennine peninsula formed the natural boundaries of a discrete cultural area where various resident cultures together constituted the roots of ancient Roman civilization. Rome's rise came hand in hand with alliances, conquests, and defeats—but it was also defined by the many different internal adaptations of these early cultures.

That the early history of Rome grows out of such a variety of cultural ingredients goes a long way toward explaining the long-standing view of Rome as a merely derivative, and therefore to some extent a second-rate, culture. What we must not overlook, however, is that the very process of integrating diverse cultures and actively reforming them into a new, supposedly "superior" cultural synthesis is itself a work of epochal creativity. And it is well to remember that even the putatively autonomous evolution of the ancient Greek culture could hardly have taken place without input from local traditions as well as some adaptation from the high cultures of Phoenicia, Egypt, and the Orient.

If we look at the Apennine peninsula circa 500 BC, we see three emerging concentrations of settlement. Far to the north, the Celtic-Gallic tribes had established themselves in the area of the upper Italian lakes and the southern Alps. To the south of this, the Etruscans inhabited the region stretching from Bologna to Rome. Although the Etruscans at times reached as far to the southeast as the Campania, they were in general oriented westward toward the Tyrrhenian Sea. From Naples southward, settlement was characterized by the Greek colonial cities that had been established here and elsewhere on Mediterranean coasts from the 8th century BC. Overpopulation, crop failures, and fundamental social breakdowns had pushed the Greeks beyond their borders seeking land in foreign parts. Even if these colonies only rarely maintained intensive long-term contact with their individual mother cities, they were nonetheless oriented, with only a few exceptions, eastward toward the Greek cultural domain.

But Italy's actual cultural environment was more complex than this preliminary overview suggests. Like the Celtic-Gallic tribes, the Greeks were immigrants. Whether or not this was true of the Etruscans is unclear, but in any case the word "immigration" is a euphemism because the territory involved was not uninhabited. For the population already settled here—who had themselves wandered in from the north centuries before—the arrival of newcomers was seldom a peaceful process; on the contrary, it almost invariably prompted a desperate defensive struggle. The Greek settlement of Sicily, for example, was a particularly bloody process; the Greek historian Thucydides offers a rather offhanded recitation of the series of conquests that led up to the Greeks' ultimate victory: "Archias, a man of the Herculean family, carried a colony from Corinth and became

1   Greek colonies in Italy: The famous temple of Poseidon, erected ca. 470 BC, stood at the center of the colonial city Paestum.

2   Italy, ca. 500 BC: The Apennine peninsula was settled by several different cultures who were either conquered or gradually assimilated by Rome.

3 Found in a tomb near Canosa in Apulia, this Celtic decorative helmet is proof of the cultural intertwinings of the 4th century BC. Berlin, Antikenmuseum.

founder of Syracuse, where first he drove the Siculi out of that island. ... And in process of time, when the city was taken in with a wall, it became populous. In the fifth year after the building of Syracuse, Thucles and the Chalcideans, going from Naxos, built Leontium, expelling thence the Siculi, and after that Catana. ... The name of the city was at first Zancle, so named by the Sicilians because it hath the shape of a sickle. ... But these inhabitants were afterwards chased thence by the Samians ... After this, Anaxilas, tyrant of Rhegium, drove out the Samians, and peopling the city with a mixed people ... instead of Zancle called the place by the name of his own country." (Thucydides, *History of the Peloponnesian War*, Book VI, 3–6).

While the Etruscans settled over a broad region and either assimilated or completely drove out the other cultures of northern Italy, the Greek colonists in fact claimed only a narrow coastal strip of the peninsula for their settlements, the *poleis*; each *polis* claimed a certain amount of *chora*, or surrounding farmland. The native peoples were either enslaved, forced into the colonial settlements as social inferiors, or driven into the interior. Thus, away from the coasts and south of the Etruscans, a variety of highly diverse ethnic groups were compressed within a small area: Lapygians, Daunians, Messapians, and Apuli on the Adriatic coast; Volsci, Faliscans, Latins, Sabines, Vestini, Marsi, Aequi, and Umbri in the soon overpopulated central

4 Bronze statuette of a Campanian-Samnite warrior. Paris, Louvre.

Italy; Samnites and Osci in Campania; Lucani in the Basilicata and Bruttii in Calabria.

Today it is clear from archeological evidence—largely documented in the regional museums of the different Italian provincial cities—that most of these ethnic groups had their own individual cultures, although little is known about the groups historically. What is clear is that, between these tribes and the Etruscan-Greek culture, there were many conflicts over farmland, trade routes, and strategic positions. It is also clear that ancient Rome grew out of just such initially inconspicuous seeds in central Italy.

The Etruscans: Religion, state, economy, society

Etruscan archeological finds in Italy date back to the Villanova culture of around 1000 BC (the name comes from the site of an important archeological find near Bologna). But whether the Etruscans should be counted among the indigenous peoples of the peninsula or among the immigrants remains unclear, and subject to ongoing debate. The Etruscans, who with the Greek settlers of southern Italy left deep marks on the later ancient Roman culture, lived in the area of southern Tuscany between Fiesole and Veii from the 8th to the 1st centuries BC, and dominated Rome and its immediate surroundings until 500 BC. Our knowledge of the Etruscans derives largely from archeological finds. Ancient texts convey only a very small amount of information, a problem arising in part from the scanty

1000 – 500 BC

5 The Villanova culture preceded the Etruscans in northern and middle Italy. 9th century BC pottery from a tomb near Tarquinia. Florence, Archaeological Museum.

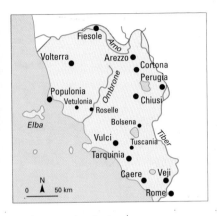

6 The Etruscan heartland, 5th century BC.

knowledge of the Etruscan script (see p. 15).

The landscape of Etruria, like that of Greece, is very disjointed. As a result, the 8th century BC brought a settlement pattern in which several core villages were combined into autonomous city-states bounded by natural agricultural areas. The Etruscan city-states, unlike the Greek, early united into a federation that was ruled by the twelve most powerful settlements and that maintained relative peace among the members. The center of the federation was the Voltumna shrine in the area of Volsinii (Bolsena). The 6th and 5th centuries BC followed with further Etruscan city-state federations into the Po valley and Campania.

In the Etruscan heartland, where most of the cities were located, the large settlements were situated on plateaus that offered easy and natural fortification—they were only approachable from one side and were linked by a network of roads. The layouts of the settlements, as demonstrated particularly well by the new excavations of Marzabotto, were spread out, with a rectangular street network uniting the spacious atrium houses—precursors of the later Roman townhouses (see p. 68ff)—with public buildings and plazas. The religious center was typically the three-roomed podium temple (see p. 18ff). The necropolises, which have been generally better preserved than the settlements, were always located outside the cities, and were themselves literal cities of the dead.

7 Like the original Etruscan settlement, the modern city of Orvieto lies on a large, strategic plateau with steep sides.

8 "Industrial area" near Populonia: The mining and smelting of ores was an important element in the Etruscan economy.

The economic basis of this advanced culture rested on the abundance of ore that was exploited after around 800 BC. At the same time, the Etruscans used their strategic bridge position in the Mediterranean to establish themselves as important traders, and many cities along the coast had well developed harbors. The Etruscan culture distinguished itself with its unreserved openness to other cultures. Archeological finds bear witness to contacts with the Phoenicians on the Levantine coast as far as Carthage, to the Ionians of Asia Minor, the Greeks, Thracians, Anatolians, and, closer to home, to Corsica, Sardinia, the Province and almost all of the other cultures of the Apennine peninsula. The vast majority of Greek pottery vases filling museums around the world came from Etruscan tombs, indicating that they were Greek exports to the region (12).

The Etruscans were engaged not only in trade with raw materials and foreign products but also in their own areas of production. Master goldsmiths and metallurgists, the Etruscans successfully copied the painted clay vases of the Greeks, and exported black lacquered *Bucchero* ceramics, a skillfully made imitation of expensive metallic vessels.

The considerable differences in the size and appointments of Etruscan tombs suggest an oligarchic, aristocratic social structure within the individual settlements. Each settlement was apparently headed by a king or local prince from what was probably a numerically small nobility who were the sole owners of the land. There has often been speculation about initiatives dating from the 6th and 5th centuries BC toward a republican structure, as seem to have been made in Rome during the same period, but such an inference is problematic because the factual early history of Rome is also largely unknown.

That Etruscan culture was fairly receptive to a wide variety of influences is especially clear in its religion, which consisted of a complex synthesis of both original and "foreign" Greek, Latin, and Phoenician-Oriental deities. Imparted by prophets and inscribed in books, the Etruscan religion bears some similarity to Judaism, except that it incorporated an extraordinarily large number of deities. Even the organization of the inner rooms of the temples into three almost equivalent cult areas points to the comparatively equalizing tendency of the Etruscan divine cosmos.

Minutely regulated rites were prescribed for almost all aspects of life. Whether founding a city or building a city wall, prescriptions were to be followed and priests were to be present to see that they were. Science and technology were bound into the ritual system—the cosmic interpretation of the heavens and weather patterns, analysis of birds' flights, or "reading" of the intestines and liver were components of the Etruscans' extremely regimented religious practices. The Roman philosopher and playwright Seneca,

9 Bronze imitation of a sheep's liver containing characters—possibly an educational tool for learning the ritual of organ reading. Piacenza, Museum.

10 The mummy bindings from Zagreb (Museum) were torn from an Etruscan book of linen that probably served in the 1st century BC as a festival calendar with instructions for performing cult rituals.

11 The small gold plates of Pyrgi (near Cerveteri) consecrated to the goddess Astarte. Etruscan text (middle and bottom), Phoenician text (top), ca. 500 BC. Rome, Villa Giulia.

who was the teacher of the emperor Nero, offered a graphic description of this scientizing of religion: "The [Etruscan] knowledge of lightning was organized in three phases: that of research, that of hands-on practice, and that of propitiation. The first is a matter of system, the second of divination, the third of atonement to the gods." (*Natural Questions*, 2, 33).

The Etruscan script

Perhaps the chief reason why so little is known of Etruscan society, and why so many myths abound today, is that Etruscan writing is still very much an unsolved riddle. Etruscan is an alphabetic script, as opposed to a syllabic or word script. Similar in many respects to eastern Greek dialects, its letters are even readable—but its vocabulary is not: Rather, the meaning of the words remains for the most part unknown.

There are approximately 7,500 known Etruscan texts, most of them very short, containing only names and offices, for example, from grave inscriptions. What we lack are longer texts written in parallel languages—something like the famous Rosetta Stone (now in the British Museum) that enabled Jean François Champollion to decipher Egyptian hieroglyphs in 1822. Even if modern linguistics pretends to a quite precise knowledge of Etruscan, the few lengthy epigraphic artifacts of this culture, such as the strips of an Etruscan feast calendar later used to wrap a mummy (**10**), have still only been partially translated, and the single factually

1000 – 500 BC

12 Most painted Greek vases that are today museum showpieces were found in Etruscan tombs and may have been made as cheap imitations of more elaborate metal vessels. The so-called Nikosthenes amphora from Athens, ca. 530 BC. Rome, Villa Giulia.

13 The necropolis of Cerveteri, a large city of the dead; tumuli, or barrows, dating from the 7th or 6th century BC.

informative inscription of any length, the gold plates of Pyrgi (11), translates the Etruscan into another only partially understood language, Phoenician. Thus, like the Minoan Linear-B, Etruscan writing remains a challenge for scholars.

Etruscan tombs as a mirror of life

Until now, excavations of individual Etruscan settlements have yielded little exact knowledge of daily life in an Etruscan household—the standards of furnishings and equipment, the number of rooms and the organization of living space, the manufacture and variation of form and function of household equipment. In fact, the foundations of many houses and urban structures that are mostly those of Etruscan cities have survived, such as Orvieto (7), but because the sites have been continuously settled from antiquity to the present, the excavations are seldom able to convey a direct picture of the golden age of the Etruscans from the 7th to the 3rd centuries BC.

Etruscan tombs, on the other hand, offer a strikingly clear mirror of life; the well-preserved necropolises of Vulci, Tarquinia, and Cerveteri in particular shed considerable light upon almost all aspects of Etruscan life. For one thing, the jewelry and implements that were buried with the dead as grave offerings indicate in many cases considerable wealth. In addition to great quantities of painted Greek vases, these cities of the dead have yielded up elaborately granulated

gold jewelry, decoratively carved metal objects including original furnishings such as bronze beds, lamps, and tables, small ivory plates with patterns in relief, as well as quantities of sumptuously decorated—but probably merely decorative—weapons. It is hard to avoid drawing from this evidence the impression of great wealth, at least among the nobility. One may fairly assume that only a small portion of such valuable items were spared from life on this side of the grave to serve as burial gifts.

But Etruscan tombs indicate more about daily life than is directly suggested by such burial gifts. The large tumuli of the necropolis of Cerveteri, which at times reach as much as 130 feet in diameter, cover one or more burial chambers built of tuff stone. These chambers in turn house several graves and thus were probably family tombs consisting of several rooms clustered around a corridor. It is likely that the room arrangement replicated the interior of actual houses. Architectural details down to the methods of construction are carved into the soft volcanic rock: columns with capitals capped with beams, complete wall constructions with cornices, socle areas, windows, doors, and niches, intricately detailed roof structures with ridge beams, gable sheathing, and wooden rafters extending to the walls.

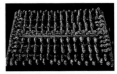

14 Engraved golden fibula (garment pin) from a grave near Palestrina, ca. 675 BC. Rome, Villa Giulia.

1000 – 500 BC

15 Tomb as living quarters: The *tomba dei rilievi* in Cerveteri is a copy of an Etruscan house with alcoves, roof, and furnishings.

16 Bronze mirrors like this one from Populonia were often placed in Etruscan tombs as funeral gifts in the 5th and 4th centuries BC.

Furniture was also re-created out of tuff stone. Lounging divans and throne-like chairs stand in individual "rooms," as does the coffin of the dead, either in the form of simple boxes set on the stone couches or, in the more elaborate settings, the coffins are made of terra cotta in the form of a sofa or a magnificent bed. The particularly richly appointed tombs pass over such stone or clay imitations entirely; instead, the chambers are furnished with expensive original pieces of ivory-clad bronze and upholstered furniture.

Like an actual city, the necropolis was laid out with broad main streets and narrower side-streets. Each burial chamber was accessible by such paths and thus available for later burials. A solid but movable stone door was set across the entrance, and the door beam was often inscribed with the family name and details of any particularly famous deeds or political or religious offices held by the family. Burials also offered the surviving family an opportunity to show off the magnificence of their tomb facilities—and thereby their earthly wealth—via elaborate burial processions: The splendor of the tomb thus was an indicator of the family's social position.

The Tuscan-Roman temple

The Etruscan temple, called "Tuscan" by the Roman architect Vitruvius in his *de architectura libri decem* (Ten Books of Architecture), was fundamentally different from the long, flat, rect-angular Greek temple with its regular columns and terraced construction. The Etruscan model was an upright structure with a wide stoop on the side of the entrance. Built into this strongly compressed, box-like, sometimes almost square form was the actual temple building, the *cella*. Full round columns stood only in front of the

17 Clay model of a 2nd-century BC Etruscan temple from Vulci. Rome, Villa Giulia.

temple; the other sides had molded half-columns. The Tuscan column, a fourth classification along with the Doric, Ionic, and Corinthian, is in fact reminiscent of the Doric design, but has a base and lacks the typical Doric entablature with its metopes and triglyphs. The interior of the cella was normally divided into three sections, to serve a trinity of gods rather than a single deity.

The Romans appropriated wholesale this Etruscan concept of a front-oriented podium temple without a surrounding crown of free-standing columns. The central forums in almost every Roman city contained such a temple— the best example is the so-called "Maison Carrée" in Nîmes, France. Later, Etruscan-Tuscan building principles were supplanted largely by the Corinthian, more rarely by the Ionic, and in rare cases by the Doric, but during the Roman period the building of "Greek" temples remained more the exception than the rule.

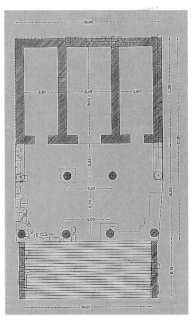

1000 – 500 BC

18 Floor plan of the Etruscan temple at Orvieto, 5th century BC, with open stairs, a podium, and the three-room *cella* as its architectural center.

19 Foundation of the podium of the temple at Talamone, 4th century BC.

The Roman Religion

The Roman religion was a complex mixture of Greek, Etruscan, and native Latin elements, and was an integral aspect of the founding mythos of the city. Together, the religious rites, the forms of the gods, and the myths of origin comprised a logical and harmonious synthesis of the various strands of legends. Religion may be viewed as both a shared myth of a society and an indirect mirror of ongoing historical processes. The manner and means by which the Greek gods were transformed by the interworkings of Etruscan magic (such as auspices, augury, and the reading of organs) with motifs of Greek mythology (for example, the foundation legends involving the legends of Aeneas and the Trojan War) make it clear that a multi-faceted network of extremely varied cultural components was woven over the course of the centuries. It was meant to mask historical gaps, provide continuity, explain the present directly by means of the mythical past, and thus bind together both the internal social identity and the relationship with the outside world.

The Etruscan features of the Roman religion are readily apparent in the many rituals relating to the household and rural life. An Etruscan religious sensibility underlies many Roman phenomena such as the cults and rites for the protection of house and farmyard, field and harvest—like the worship of the Penates and Lares (household gods)—magical rituals and festivals, certain prophetic elements such as the Sibylline Books, the pedantic regimentation of ritual practices, and the complex organization of the priesthood and its relationship to public and state life.

Etruscan influence is also evident in the funereal war games that formed the seed of the later gladiatorial contests (see p. 67ff), as well as in the triad of Jupiter, Juno, and Minerva as the divine crown of the heavenly realm and the ritual community of the main temple. But, of course, here many elements of Greek mythology and religious

20 Jupiter was the highest of the Roman divinities and corresponded to the Greek god Zeus. Bronze statuette from the middle of the 1st century AD. Malibu, CA, J. P. Getty Museum.

The Roman Religion

21 The time-honored sacrifice of the *Suovetaurilia*, in which a bull, a ram, and a boar were ritually led in a circle before they were slaughtered. Relief from the pedestal of a monument in the Forum Romanum, 303 AD.

practice are also evident. Elaborately staged games were already described by Homer, for example at the funeral for the Greek hero Patroclos who had fallen in the struggle for Troy; such practices were also common in Thrace and Asia Minor. The main Roman gods themselves were only rarely original to Rome; most corresponded to Etruscan deities, like the double-headed Janus, or to the Greek, such as the pairings Jupiter-Zeus, Juno-Hera, Neptune-Poseidon, Minerva-Athena, Diana-Artemis, Aesculapius-Asklepios, Mars-Ares, Mercury-Hermes, Venus-Aphrodite, Vulcan-Hephaestus, and Ceres-Demeter. Occasionally, a Greek god was adopted without a name change, such as Apollo.

While the Roman versions of the Greek deities are most familiar to the average person today, there were many other deities that point to a specifically Roman religious feature: the cult of values and properties. Ubiquitous were personifications of Honos (honor), Virtus (courage), Fides (loyalty), Concordia (harmony), Fortuna (luck), and Victoria (victory). The deification of such qualities, often served with their own shrines, is unique to Roman religion.

The many layers of the Roman religion itself and its rich relationship with other ancient religious concepts cannot all be addressed here. Nonetheless, the religion of Rome offers a dynamic and complex picture

The Roman Religion

22 Shrine for the *lares* in the House of the Vettii in Pompeii, between 63 and 79 AD. Rather than the traditional niche containing statues, such a flat, painted, stucco-ornamented niche often served the household rituals of the *lares*. The lord of the house is in the middle, placed above the snake and between two protective *lares*.

that changed as the nation expanded, and hence, the history of the religion reflects the history of the nation. As the Romans conquered new lands and subsumed new cultures, the conquered peoples linked their myths with those of Rome. By the time of Augustus, a totally new organization of the cults had taken place, and by no later than the 2nd century AD, both the spread of Christianity and the popularity of eastern-Oriental and Semitic religions produced a multifarious syncretism which, in spite of many prohibitions and persecutions, effectively turned the ancient Roman religious system into a conglomerate of all the

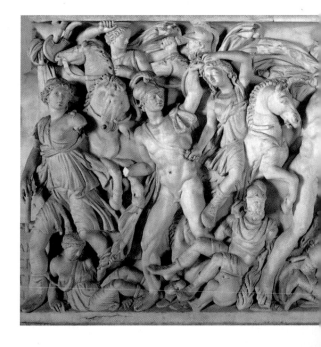

The Roman Religion

various religions practiced in the realm. With the establishment of monotheistic Christianity as the state religion (325 AD), the (from the Christian point of view) "heathen" practices of the other religions were forcibly stopped by law, dispossession, and often brutal persecution.

24 Sadism is a central motif in Roman culture, appearing in many religious practices and illustrations. This scene from a mystery cult depicts a young naked girl being whipped with switches. Wall painting from the Villa of the Mysteries in Pompeii, ca. 30 BC.

23 In the Roman era, Greek myths were severely re-tailored to the Roman needs for public display. This ca. 240 AD sarcophagus depicting a battle against the Amazons allows the Roman couple (sporting a fashionable 3rd-century AD hairstyle) to be incorporated into the popular motif of Achilles and Penthesilea. The theme is no longer the Amazon battle; it is instead the self-glorification of the tomb owners. Rome, Vatican.

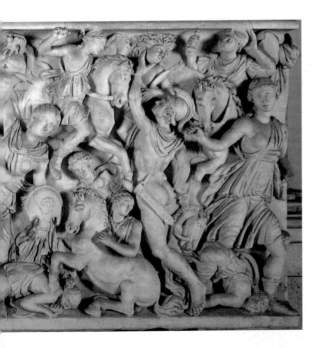

The founding of Rome and the time of the kings

25 The Capitoline Wolf nursing the twins Romulus and Remus. The wolf is a bronze statue dating from the 5th century BC, but the twins are a contribution of the Renaissance modeled after ancient coins. Rome, Conservators Palace.

700 – 27 BC

514 Illumination of Siddhartha; founding of Buddhism

510–507 Overthrow of Athenian tyranny; reforms of Cleisthenes as the first step toward democracy

490–479 Greek wars against the Persians and Phoenicians

479 Death of Confucius

338 Battle at Chaeronea; Greece falls under Macedonian domination

323 Death of Alexander the Great

312 Construction of the Appian Way as the first transregional road in Italy

ca. 300 Legendary Chinese philosopher Lao-tze writes the *Tao-te-ching*

268 First silver coins minted in Rome

221–210 Ch'in Dynasty: construction of the Great Wall begins

212–211 Siege, conquest, and plundering of Syracuse

210 Transfer of Greek art works from Capua to Rome

209 Plundering of Tarentum

168 Triumphal procession of Aemilius Paullus through Rome after his conquest of Greece; public display of plundered Greek art

The legendary founding of the city of Rome by the twin brothers Romulus and Remus, illegitimate but noble foundlings raised by a wolf, was described by the Greek writer Plutarch in the 2nd century AD: "After gathering many people to them, they determined to build a city there on the spot where they had grown up. As Romulus and Remus were about to lay the foundations, an argument broke out between them. They agreed to settle the dispute by an observation of birds. Six birds appeared to Remus, but supposedly twice as many to Romulus. But many say that Romulus lied. Remus felt betrayed and was in the end killed by Romulus in a fight. Romulus buried Remus and founded the city, to which he allowed the Etruscans entry for they provided ritual instructions on all things. Romulus defined the boundary of the city by plowing a circle: Within one day he drew a deep furrow around the seven hills and thus determined the course of the city wall and its gates. This was called the *pomerium*.

"Then he gathered all the men capable of carrying weapons and divided them into legions; he declared them all citizens, and the 100 most capable, the council (Senate). In the fourth month after its founding, the capture of the Sabine women was undertaken (Rape of the Sabine Women). ... They also set up an asylum for all refugees, and thus the new city filled up quickly." (*Romulus*, 9–14).

From this and a great variety of similar surviving founding myths, Romulus emerged as the first of seven kings of—entirely apocryphal—

legendary fame: he was succeeded by Numa Pompilius, Tullius Hostilius, Ancus Marcius, Tarquinius Priscus, Servius Tullius, and Tarquinius Superbus before the Etruscans were overcome around 500 BC by the equally legendary Brutus (**29**), who replaced the monarchy with a republic and established the consular system.

Using mythological references, attempts were made even in ancient times to compute the exact date of the founding of Rome. The best-known of such dates is that of Varro, who put Rome's founding at 753 BC; others, however—calculated by Timaios, 814–815; Cato, 752–751; Fabius Pictor, 748–747; and Cincius, 729–728—have come down through the millenia, each based on different premises drawn from Rome's official annals. These efforts to pinpoint the city's origin in time issue not from mere curiosity but from a desire to establish the credibility of the annals and to bring them into accord with Greek historiography, the numeration of the Olympiades and the Athenian archons.

Archeological excavation from the city's prehistoric period yields a rather less impressive picture, but even this kind of evidence is far from unambiguous. The total area of the city, after all, was repeatedly built upon, and this muddies the evidence and has provoked innumerable disputes among scholars. It was probably not until around 1000 BC—that is, relatively late and well beyond the gray mist of pre-history—that first the Palatine

134	Tiberius Sempronius Gracchus becomes People's Tribune; he is assassinated in 133
123	Gaius Sempronius Gracchus becomes People's Tribune; he is assassinated in 121
113–101	War against the Cimbri and Teutones; Roman defeats at Noreia (113) and Arausio (105); victories of Marius at Aquae Sextiae (102) and Vercellae (101)
73–71	Spartacus uprising; Verres is governor in Sicily
70	Cicero's diatribe against Verres, who goes into voluntary exile
63	Cicero as consul; Catiline conspiracy

700 – 27 BC

26 *Rape of the Sabine Women.* Oil painting by Jacques-Louis David, 1799. Paris, Louvre.

25

and the Quirinal and, later, the other five hills were settled by an Iron Age culture for which both cremation and burial were common—a culture thus probably constituted by a mixture of indigenous and immigrant ethnic groups. Their cemeteries were located on the grounds of the later Forum Romanum. Around 700 BC, these previously loosely connected hill settlements united into a community like a city. This merging of various settlements into a single community required a newly organized infrastructure—for example, it demanded establishment of common shrines and gathering places, construction of common fortifications, and removal of the necropolis to another location.

Contrary to legend, this was not an autonomous process; rather, it came about under Etruscan hegemony. It is even possible that early Rome was itself an Etruscan settlement. This particular theory is supported by evidence that Etruscan rituals were included in the

27 Rome as a village: Model of the Iron Age settlement on the Palatine, ca. 800 BC.

foundation of the city (for example, the specific location of the city was demarcated according to an augury ritual), and by long-term retention of many different Etruscan symbols of honor and rank including the *fasces*, the emblematic bundle of rods carried by the lictors (middle-ranked public servants in the Roman hierarchy), and the *sella curulis*, the imposing formal seat of justice, a folding chair made of ivory for the chief magistrate of justice (**182**). These artifacts and customs, as well as the purple toga worn by the army commander, were all borrowings from Etruscan culture.

The very heart of the early Roman patriarchal and hierarchical structure of the state derives

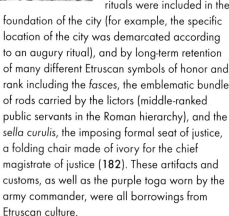

from the Etruscan culture. The population was divided into the *gentes*—the property-owning aristocratic clans—and the *clientes*—free but un-propertied plebeians who were dependent on the gentes. The gentes were organized into three groups, each comprised of ten *curiae*. The meeting of all thirty *comitiae* constituted the public assembly; the same tripartite structure was found in the organization of the military as well.

From village to state: Confederations, wars, and the Republic as a model of sovereignty

There is no doubt that the legends about the founding of Rome and the early monarchy are the products of efforts to rewrite history as myth, but the point at which myth resolves back into more objective history of Rome's earliest days remains unclear. The ancient traditions of annal writing and historiography are riddled with euphemism and revisionist harmonizing truth with myth—so much so that the early historians of Rome are among the earliest promulgators of "disinformation" as they consciously handed down western civilization's first known instances of historical falsification. In 1957, historian Plinio Fraccaro commented, with a touch of resigna-tion, that "the greatest virtue in research on the history of early Rome is the ability to push aside the majority of the surviving reports; in second place is the ability to inter-pret the rest as logically as possible."

Around 500 BC, with the banishment of the Tar-quinian Etruscans, Rome first stepped out from under the Etruscan shadow and emerged into the light of history as a power in its own right. The 430

28 Roman territory (red), colonies and allies (yellow), ca. 250 BC: The former Etruscan city-state dominated all of central and southern Italy.

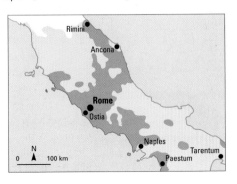

700 – 27 BC

29 Bronze bust of a Roman, 300 BC. The portrait has often been assumed (probably incorrectly) to be of the founder and first consul of the Republic, Lucius Iunius Brutus. Rome, Conservators' Palace.

30 Marble frieze from the temple of Apollo in the Marcellus theater in Rome, ca. 20 BC (segment). The frieze shows a triumphal procession displaying war booty to the population of Rome. On the litter are a trophy of victory and two prisoners, and behind, a trumpeter. Rome, Conservators' Palace.

hectares circumscribed by the city wall had already allowed this particular settlement to outstrip the other Etruscan settlements in size. Its initial policy was to adopt the procedures of its northern neighbor: alliance with other settlements and—only as a second and final means—war and suppression. Like the Etruscan city federation, a Latin alliance arose. The role and status of Rome in this early period of the alliance is unknown, but at the beginning of the 4th century BC, there were a series of wars with the immediate neighbors; the result was Rome's emergence as the ruling power of central Italy. Later in the century, Rome instigated another series of wars conducted in various constellations of alliances that reached beyond the region of central Italy, and the city quickly grew into an influential state on the threshold of world political power.

This rapid process of transformation from a small, dependent settlement to a powerful political entity that would radically change the structures of the entire Mediterranean world in fewer than five centuries was bound to have consequences, both for the world at large and for the internal structures of the state itself. Where once noble families ruled over their own

limited territories, they now were obliged to organize themselves and divide their labor; and whatever they did necessarily involved and affected the plebeians—the "common" population. The ascendancy of the Republic over the royal hegemony was also mythologized and ascribed in the annals to Brutus (**29**), who, as the first consul, introduced the consul lists. In fact, this new republican form of state entailed an elaborately complex organization based on constitutional principles; on the one hand, the Republic boasted a regionally organized military structure, and on the other hand, it stood on a foundation of a class system defined by property ownership. The form of the Republic evolved not overnight by dictum or decision, but over decades amid much conflict. Both aspects of the Republic—the military and the class system—were at first characterized by great social gaps between the patricians and the plebeians; well into the 1st century BC, there were recurrent war-like civil disturbances that successively granted participation in the political process to the less-privileged groups (see p. 34).

31 The rostra in the Forum Romanum was both an institutional and an architectural symbol of the Republic. From time immemorial, the bronze prows of ships captured in sea battles (lat. *rostrum*) were mounted on the stand as trophies. Reconstructive drawing, 1905.

700 – 27 BC

The most important state offices in the Roman Republic can be traced back as far as the 5th century BC. Two consuls, elected annually by the public assembly, were responsible for the state's military and civil power. Another range of officials—some elected, some appointed by consuls—included the *quaestors*, *censors*, and later the *praetors* and *aediles*, who together embodied the different, separate functions of the erstwhile consular authority. These officials made up the extended level of upper magistrates around which other administrative officials were organized.

During the 4th and 5th centuries BC, in time of war, the two consuls were often replaced by a college of up to six representatives

32 Roman magistrates wearing togas, symbols of their rank. Fragment of a bronze relief. Malibu, CA, J. P. Getty Museum.

elected to occupy all the necessary posts of command. There was also the already long influential "council of elders," or Senate, in which only the *gentes*, the patrician families, had seats and votes. This Senate was an advisory body for the consuls, but in practice, its authority prevented the consuls from ignoring its advice.

Internal strife within the Republic, which was characteristic throughout its history, did not prevent the Romans from seeing their state as the model for all other peoples. In modern analysis, the history of early Rome is a chronicle of the development of a governmental and administrative form that was, by virtue of its considerable flexibility and intrinsic tendency to permanent compromise, at first ideally suited to handle the geographic growth of the state and the ensuing variety of new administrative tasks. In the end, however, the Republic foundered in the wake of ever more quickly advancing territorial expansion.

Rome between the aristocracy and the people: Social crises and their significance for the republican state

From its beginning, the Roman Republic was marked by bloody internal conflicts. Even if the details of the transition from a hereditary monarchy to a republican state remain largely shrouded in mystery, the mere fact that such a transition took place suggests that, sometime around 500 BC, some situation demanded the participation of broader circles in political authority. The reason for this may lie—as in Greece several generations earlier—in the need for a broad-based and reliable military; if this is in fact the cause, then the very seed of the Republic lay in the organized army with its committees and elections.

The period between 494 and 366 BC was marked by class conflicts during which the plebeians, who had been drawn into the military organization, were able to extract, by force, wider-reaching rights from the patricians. That such enfranchisement was secured only under pressure is clear from the beginning of the conflict: In one spectacular demonstration, the plebeians abandoned the city. This act clearly demonstrated to the nobility the seriousness of the plebeians' demands for improvements in their legal and economic status, and simultaneously showed the patricians just how vulnerable their city was. Only in response to this massive threat to the state's security did the patricians concede certain improvements, such as the establishment of plebeian assemblies and special state offices (peoples' tribune and *aediles*). Finally, after further struggle, the compromise was sealed by two laws, the Twelve Tables (ca. 450 BC) and the Licinian-Sextian Law from 367 BC. Together, the laws provided for economic, social, legal, and political balance through measures such as debt adjustment, plebeian qualification for the consulate, establishment of a "meritocracy" drawn from both plebeians and patricians, and the written codification of private, penal, and process law to assure fair application of the law to all.

The rapid growth in size of the Roman state was also necessarily attended by social complications. It did not take long for a clear division to arise between the real "Romans"— that is, the political elite—and the "others"—the inhabitants of the annexed territories. Some clearly defined organizational system was going to be needed to manage community life in in the state's ever-growing territory.

33 Roman citizen making a rhetorical gesture. According to the inscription on the hem of the toga, a public monument for Aulus Metellius. Ca. 80 BC. Florence, Archaeological Museum.

34 The war and trade harbor of Puteoli on the Gulf of Naples was the most important harbor on the west coast of Italy before the completion of Ostia at the mouth of the Tiber. Wall painting from Stabiae, ca. 50 AD. Naples, National Museum.

The navy played a very important role in Rome's rise to a world power, but not in the early years. As a federation that was also engaged in sea trade, Rome initially relied at sea, as on land, on the tried and trusted principle of alliances to keep the necessary travel routes open. It was not until after 260 BC, in the face of growing conflict with the colonial power of Carthage that would become the First Punic War, and when Rome began its attempts to intervene in Sicily, that Rome begin to build its own fleet. In a mere 100 years, this fleet developed into a force that ruled the Mediterranean and was a fundamental military component of Roman expansion.

Initially the Roman navy was commanded by the two consuls; later, it fell under the aegis of a praetor or legate. The commander possessed broad powers but was also held directly accountable for the fate of those under his command. It was the commander's duty after a battle, for example, to recover the bodies of his fallen sailors and convey them back to Rome.

The fleet consisted of squadrons of various types of ships that were oared in battle to maximize moveability. The oarsmen were fully trained soldiers—only as an exception were they slaves or prisoners of war. The safety of the ship and the fighting power that would ultimately decide the outcome of a sea battle depended on the abilities of the soldiers. Longer voyages without battles were undertaken under sail. During the period of the Republic, squadrons were recruited only when necessary. It was not until the age of Augustus that permanent

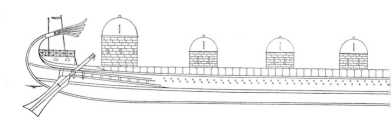

The Roman Navy

fleets were stationed in harbors around the Mediterranean.

Naval operations in the ancient world almost invariably followed the pattern of martial strategy on land. Naturally, the goal was to ram and sink the enemy ships. Most often, however, enemy ships were boarded sideways over portable bridges carried on board, while the ships were anchored with the newly invented grapnel; the troops were then engaged in deck maneuvers that resembled close-quarter combat on land. For this purpose, ships were often specially outfitted with turrets and palisades. Most skirmishes took place along the coast and were supported by troops on land, with the commanding officer directing the movement of ships from an elevated vantage point on shore. The navy also conducted operations on the open sea and developed tactical innovations supported by the ships' long-range weapons. Captured ships were burned on land in a triumphal rite, and the bronze ramming heads were removed and displayed as trophies (**36**).

36 Victory monument built from the prows of enemy ships, erected by Augustus at the site of the sea battle of Actium (31 BC). Reconstruction.

In the same measure that the *classis romana*—the official name of the Roman fleet—was expanded and stationed in assigned harbors, its military significance disappeared. The last great campaign of conquest was the landing in Britain in 55 BC; after this, with just a few exceptions and continued use to combat pirates, the navy's only marked military role came in the civil wars after the assassination of Julius Caesar. The sea battle of Actium in 31 BC in which Augustus defeated Mark Antony and laid the foundation for a new monarchy was, as a propaganda tool, a crowning glory for Augustus—but it also marked in a sense the end of the navy.

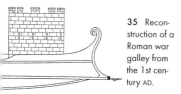

35 Reconstruction of a Roman war galley from the 1st century AD.

37 Roman with ancestral busts. Such plaster heads were molded from death masks and were probably the predecessors of Roman portraits. Ancestral images functioned as models and reference points for the present generation. Rome, Conservators Palace.

One distinction—quickly considered discriminatory—was citizenship. Citizenship at first pertained only to the inhabitants of the city-state of Rome, its immediate surroundings, and the colonial cities founded directly by Rome on conquered land. All other communities under Roman jurisdiction possessed a second-class citizenship without voting rights. And the largest portion of the newly won territories were designated as confederates or allies; these areas were bound to Rome by treaty and allowed administrative autonomy, but their own governments had to recognize all Roman decisions and to acknowledge their territory as *ager publicus*, that is, public land of Rome.

Even these arrangements, however, were unable to keep pace with the rapid expansion of the state in the 3rd and 2nd centuries BC. In return for military service, more and more veterans had to be settled in the *ager publicus*, but this only gave rise to more conflicts with both the patricians who farmed the land and the land's original owners. Under such circumstances, the inhabitants of Italy demanded Roman citizenship with increasing force and, with it, a voice in all arenas of government. In the years following 133 BC, after the brothers Tiberius and Gaius Gracchus failed in their attempts to reform the Republic in the face of embittered patrician opposition, the tensions resulted in a long civil war with very complicated military and legal constellations.

Where the social conflict involved with the class struggles of the 5th and 4th cen-

38 Plaster death mask as model for a bust. Cairo, Archaeological Museum.

turies BC had ultimately strengthened the republican constitution and garnered the support of the general population, all of which brought the system increased stability, external expansion still tended to exacerbate internal dissension which could not be resolved in the climate of constant civil wars. In 89 BC citizenship was granted to all confederates of the Roman state, though this was perceived by many as an unavoidable defeat and was followed by further enforced distortions of the original Roman system. Every attempt to rectify the problems, whether through reform or dictatorship, contravened the system, making it ever less practicable. It was not until 27 BC that Augustus formally ended the civil war and, in an elaborately progapandized move, "reestablished the Republic." This was, though, mere rhetoric; by this time the Republic existed in name only; Rome was once again a de facto hereditary monarchy (see p. 44).

39 Silver denarius dating from the war between Rome and its confederates (91–89 BC). The Oscian mint depicts the Italian bull overcoming the Roman wolf.

700 – 27 BC

From a confederation of cities to dominance: Politics and the military

Whether or not it is true, as a common argument maintains, that Rome was forced unwillingly into world leadership through a series of accidents, one thing is certain: Once Rome decided on war, it proceeded with ruthless severity against its enemies. At the same time, Rome's foreign policy was generally very inconsistent. At the heart of this inconsistency was the formal legalism typical

40 The Roman highway net within Italy, ca. 150 BC. The primary purpose of Roman roads was to provide good military connections, secure newly won territories, and carry mail and other communication; commerce and travel were only secondary concerns.

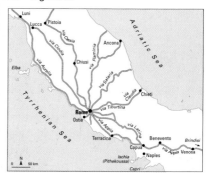

35

41 Relief from a victory monument erected in Delphi by the Roman general after the conquest of Macedonia. Delphi Museum.

42 The veterans' colony of Cosa, founded at a strategic point in 273 BC, is an early example of a Roman city that was established not only in payment for army service, but also to be a political and military support in conquered territories.

of the Roman view of the world: "The Romans never understood their history as one of conflict," writes historian Walter Eder, "but as one that marched under the banner of harmony (*concordia*). Their perception of foreign affairs must also be seen in this light: Each conquered enemy had to be 'integrated,' through defeat, annexation, or treaty. For the Romans, an outsider that was unpredictable, with whom no permanently stable relations could be formed, always signified an affliction. For this reason, the threshold for identifying danger was extremely low; and for this reason as well, Roman 'imperialism' was in principle boundless. 'Interventions,' therefore occurred with increasing regularity."

The chain of Rome's hostile actions against the increasingly unpredictable "outside world" is long, but it is by no means exclusively a chain of successes. Rome sometimes suffered defeats, even in its home territory in Italy: in 216 BC, for example, the Roman forces were overwhelmed by Hannibal's army at Cannae. Still, on the whole, events followed a clear course. The first expansion occurred in Italy, then extended to the war with Tarentum (282–272 BC) in the south to the first supraregional involvements with Hellenistic-Greek monarchies. Rome's first two Punic wars (264–241 and 218–210 BC) against its one-time close ally Carthage resulted in the conquest of Sicily, parts of Spain, and, indirectly, Sardinia and Corsica; the Third Punic War wrought the destruction of Carthage. Rome's attempts to remain aloof from the exigencies of the skirmishes among the Hellenistic monarchies in the east led to exactly the opposite effect. Rome was drawn into ever more involved war scenarios, first with Macedonia, which was conquered in 168 BC in the victory at Pydna, and then with the rest of Greece, whose conquest culminated in the destruction of Corinth in a bloody massacre in 146 BC. When the king of Pergamon in Asia Minor, Attalos III, died in 133 BC and bequeathed his kingdom to the Romans, and the victory at Numantia in Spain the same year

gave Rome the Iberian peninsula, the Mediterranean became virtually a Roman lake.

Territorial expansion demanded not only constitutional but also administrative reform. So long as expansion had been limited to central Italy, the colonial cities founded as veteran settlements on the recently gained territory were under the control of the state and held the right of citizenship. Later, administrative units were established in the form of *regiones*, which became the forerunners of the later Roman provinces. The first province administered by a Roman governor was Sicily in 241 BC, followed by Sardinia and Corsica in 227 BC, Spain in 197 BC, Africa, Macedonia, and Greece

43 Hannibal (right) and the Roman general Scipio (left) meet face to face in the Second Punic War (218 – 202 BC). Flemish tapestry of the 18th century. Rome Quirinal Palace.

Rome was generous with friends and allies, but merciless toward enemies and rebels. The Greek author Plutarch describes the occupation of Athens by Sulla's troops in 86 BC: "Sulla broke into the city at midnight and, yelling wildly, the army poured through the streets with drawn swords, set loose to rob, murder, and rape, so that the number of dead could not even be counted, but to this day only estimated by the amount of blood-soaked earth. The massacre in the marketplace alone flooded the ground with blood all the way to the Dipylon Gate, and blood is said to have streamed even into the suburbs."

Plutarch, *Biography of Sulla*, 14

(Achaea) in 148–146 BC, and the inheritance of Pergamon as the Province Asia in 133 BC. The principle of annual replacement of the provincial Roman legates was in fact modified a number of times in the course of the years, remaining nonetheless a basic pattern of Roman administration until the end of the 3rd century AD (see p. 88ff).

City and country, freedmen and slaves: The republican economy and its crises

Roman society of the 4th and 3rd centuries BC was based on an agrarian autarchy. The city-state of Rome was, like all city-states, only required to import significant amounts of food in the case of poor harvests. The aristocracy derived their status from land ownership while most people were farmers who either depended directly on the landowners or had become free landholders through the establishment of the veteran colonies. It was precisely this "middle class" that was the pillar of the republican system. It guaranteed Roman rule in the acquired territories of central Italy and played a critical role in the military.

At the same time, with the Roman advances, trade assumed such an important place in the economy that Roman agriculture was thrown into a deep crisis. When Cato, the conservative idealizer of the past, opened his *de agri cultura* around 200 BC with the declaration, "It is certain that trade is extremely profitable—if it were not so risky; and the same for lending money—if it were not so immoral ...; but among the sources of income, agriculture is and remains the most honorable and respectable," his almost desperate reference to the "good old days" must be seen as an indication of dramatic changes in the economy. With the incorporation of new productive regions and sources of raw materials, huge markets were created. In particular, the highly productive agricultural areas of Sicily, Greece, Asia Minor, and Spain turned their agricultural riches to a large extent into imports that competed with the produce of the Italian farmers at home. The huge profits of the merchants were paid for by the widespread ruin of the farmers.

The farmland of Italy, on the other hand, fell increasingly into the hands of a few large landowners who chose to pursue highly specialized, export-oriented monocultures (mostly wine and olives) and turned fertile, grain-producing land into spatially wasteful meadows for grazing. The new, huge farms did not even offer employment to the ruined small farmers, for they were worked by the growing class of slaves, who were captured and sold in Italy as war booty: In the Greek province of Epirus, for example, more than 150,000 prisoners were sold into slavery in 167 BC alone, and in the huge slave market on the island of Delos, 10,000 slaves changed owners daily. The result of the bur-

44 Plowing and sowing. Mosaic from a Roman house near Vienne in southern France. Saint-Germain-en-Laye, Museum.

45 Idyllic and bucolic transfiguration of heavy farm work—a favorite pictorial theme of the Roman upper classes. Relief from the 1st century AD. Munich, Glyptothek.

geoning slave trade was that the land, as a homeland of free farmers, was largely depleted and was replaced by an endless stream of gigantic agricultural estates.

The cities, in contrast, grew rapidly. They became the gathering places for the working classes, but also for the wealthy and ruling class. The cities were the sites of markets, commerce, service, trade, and industry, with production increasingly based on slave rather than wage labor.

The entire social organization grew gradually out of balance. The larger the number of urban poor who had to be provided for by the rich, the sharper the discrepancy between rich and poor. Money transfers necessary for equilibrium became more and more complex. The aristocratic consensus on which the state was based became more fragile in the face of diverging economic interests, and the social dynamite—discharging itself not only in radical ideas of reform, civil wars, and revolts, but also in slave uprisings, among which the Spartacus rebellion of 73–71 BC inflamed half of Italy in war—became more explosive.

Whereas the social hierarchy of nobles, freedmen, land-owning peasants, dependent peasants, freed slaves, and slaves had remained stable through hundreds of years, and with it the political system of the Republic, now the most severe distortions became evident. The peasantry sank to the level of a proletariat, while the numerous urban *liberti* (freed slaves)

In 18th- and 19th-century illustrations, attitudes toward Roman slavery oscillated between abhorrence and admiration: "The Romans held slaves since the most ancient times. ... With the increasing wealth of Rome, there were four circumstances that tended to increase slavery: the end of the (family) farming economy and the predominance of large farms (worked by slaves, preferred because they were exempt from military conscription); the luxury of life with its new and unknown needs; the need for administration because of the masses of slaves ... and only later the use of slaves for industrial purposes."

Joachim Marquardt, *The Private Life of the Romans*, (1886, 2nd edition), p. 136ff

and even slaves themselves rose to wealth by means of trade. Economic relations had less and less to do with the legal structure of society and attempts to impose legal regulations, such as a trade prohibition for senators or a cap on the amount of land ownership, were ultimately unable to prevent the breakdown of the time-honored system. The nobility mutated into an oligarchy, and in its place arose a new class of rich merchants and bankers (the so-called *homini novi*); the old, free peasantry disappeared almost entirely; production increasingly depended on cheap slave labor; and the population of all of Italy had to be integrated into the Roman social system—a morass of problems that soon became insoluble under the principles of the Republic.

46 In their social ascent, freed slaves copied the self-presentation of the Roman middle class. Tomb reliefs such as those of Popillius and Calpurnia (beginning of the 1st century AD) demonstrate a new middle-class self-awareness. Malibu, CA, J. P. Getty Museum.

Imperial Portraiture

47 The bust of Caligula in Malibu, CA (J. P. Getty Museum) is one of few specimens that survived the destruction of the *damnatio memoriae* decreed after the emperor's death.

The image of the Roman emperors was familiar to every person throughout the realm: Official statues at the Forum, inside military camps, or other places of public traffic; imprints on coins; the center point of scenic reliefs on public buildings, on medals, precious stones, cameos, and elsewhere, all carried the ruler's face before the vast numbers of his subjects. Even those who had never seen the emperor in person—which meant nearly everyone in the empire—had some concrete image of his person and administration of office by means of these portraits.

It would be misleading to suggest that an imperial portrait was an individualized work of art or a kind of chiseled marble photograph of the ruler. On the contrary: Since the "invention" of rulers' portraits with physiognomic features at the Macedonian court in the 4th century BC, the portrait had become a medium of propaganda by which a manipulated image, not the real face of the ruler, was conveyed to the public. In the days of the Roman empire, an original model was chosen with the approval of the court; replicas were then distributed to the four corners of the empire where copies were manufactured. Almost all surviving imperial portraits are such "grandchildren" of the original, which explains the often considerable variations uncovered within one type of portrait.

The official portraits depicted the Roman emperors in very different kinds of images. For example, there were three different types of portraits of Augustus (27 BC–r14 AD; **52–54**), and yet they all reveal a pedantically exact repetition in certain details such as the curls of his artfully arranged coiffure. Augustus had himself portrayed in what was perceived to be the exemplary style of classical Greek art as the guarantor of a self-proclaimed golden age. Vespasian (69–79 AD), who ascended the throne only after bloody fighting,

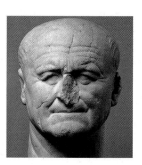

48 Vespasian. Copenhagen, Ny Carlsberg Glyptothek.

felt great pressure to legitimize his new dynasty. So he had himself portrayed in a decidedly different style—more in the tradition of private portraits of the republican period, with the worthily wrinkled face of a man engaged in honorable labors. Trajan, on the other hand (98–117 AD), preferred a military image consistent with his martial policies. Portraits of Caracalla (211–217 AD) conveyed an image of energetic body movement with eyebrows knitted together—a stolid body language meant to instill fear and respect for the emperor in the observer. Finally, the portrait of Theodosius (379–395 AD; **159**) stands in the formal and abstract tradition of Late Antiquity—removed from real life and expressive of the hierarchical distance between the ruler and the people.

The imperial Roman portrait enjoyed a certain legal status as the representative of the emperor, not unlike (in theory) the "rights" some would confer upon the American flag as proxy for "the republic for which it stands." Insults or inappropriate behavior toward official imperial likenesses were high treason. After an emperor's death, however, his portraits could be condemned to official destruction. This *damnatio memoriae* was a penal act of the Senate against emperors considered especially tyrannical or otherwise warranting official denigration. The portraits of Caligula (37–41 AD),

49 Caracalla. Copenhagen, Ny Carlsberg Glyptothek.

50 Silver denarius minted between 103 and 111 AD with a profile of Trajan. Richmond, Virginia Museum.

Nero (54–68 AD), and Domitian (81–96 AD) were all destroyed or sometimes reworked into portraits of their successors. Because the *damnatio memoriae* effectively erased the licenses of such emperors, such that very few would have survived, it is probable that the many portraits found in old art collections are not ancient; they are more likely copies made later from images on coins or gems to complete collections of Roman imperial portraits (see p. 128ff).

254-184 BC Plautus (comedies)

234-149 BC Cato, moralist and agronomist

ca. 200-120 BC Polybius, historian

170-90 BC Accius (dramas and tragedies)

106-43 BC Cicero (letters, speeches, legal writing)

95-30 BC Nepos, historian and biographer

90-ca. 20 BC Diodorus (history of the world)

87-54 BC Catullus (lyric poetry and elegies)

86-35 BC Sallust, historian

70-19 BC Virgil (*Bucolics, Georgics, Aeneid*, etc.)

65-8 BC Horace (odes and satires)

64/63 BC-ca. 23 AD Strabo, geographer

43 BC-17 AD Ovid (elegies, letters, mythological poetry, and erotica)

4 BC-65 AD Seneca, philosopher, moralist (tragedies)

23-79 AD Pliny the Elder (natural history)

30-104 AD Frontinus (text about aqueducts)

37-95 AD Flavius Josephus (Jewish historian)

40-104 AD Martial (satirical epigrams)

ca. 46-120 AD Plutarch (biographies)

ca. 55-129 AD Tacitus (*Germania, Historia*, etc.)

62-113 AD Pliny the Younger (letters)

65-128 AD Juvenal (satires)

ca. 150-200 AD Pausanias (travel report)

155-235 AD Cassius Dio, historian

175-242 AD Ammonios Sakkas, Neo-Platonism

ca. 330-ca. 395 AD Ammianus Marcellinus, historian

354-430 AD Augustine, philosopher and ethicist

27 BC – 284 AD

51   Under Caesar and Augustus, the Forum Romanum weathered the change from erstwhile political center of the Republic to the stage set for monarchy. At the eastern end of the Forum stands the temple of Caesar, flanked by two Augustan triumphal arches stretching over the main streets leading to the Forum.

Augustus—or republic lost

By the time of Julius Caesar, the Republic was already compromised by a host of separate arrangements. The first triumvirate with Pompey and Crassus (60 BC) was little more than a private agreement outside the compass of the state; similarly irregular were the years of Caesar's governorship in Gaul where his undeclared wars bore no official sanctions. In 49 BC, ignoring the ultimatum of the increasingly nervous Senate to dissolve his army and lay down all offices, Caesar instead crossed the Rubicon between Gaul and Italy fully armed, thereby from a legal perspective precipitating an open war against the state; he marched on to have himself declared dictator for life and elected consul for ten years. As so often in coups, his excuse was that he needed to save the state from destruction—Caesar never tired of posing as the guarantor of republican traditions in his anti-republican actions. When Caesar was assassinated in 44 BC, his grandnephew Gaius Octavianus—also ignoring all state institutions—set himself up as avenger and led a civil war against the murderers "in the name of the Republic." The hostilities ended only after his sea victory over Mark Antony at Actium (northwestern Greece) in

31 BC, the capture of Alexandria in 30 BC, and the consummation of various penal actions on Mark Antony's fellow travelers.

Now began a refined intrigue for power and influence. When Octavianus returned to Rome and the situation had stabilized, he ostensibly undertook the "re-creation of the Republic" with great pomp and ceremony; he also honored himself with the title *Augustus* ("exalted," "sublime"). In fact, however, nothing was the same as under the Republic, even if all was officially done under cover of justice and law—as Octavianus bestirred himself to make it appear. Without holding a single official office, referring instead to his *auctoritas*, Augustus permanently usurped an entire series of *de facto* authorities, while occasionally publicly rejecting in the style of a modest republican the proffered mandate of both Senate and people of Rome. In fact, Augustus was systematically extending a monarchical system of government that required the continual use of precisely this authority.

Thus Augustus advanced to *princeps*, the first among equals, taking possession for life of tribunal and consular powers of office without ever becoming either tribune or consul, assuming the title of *pontifex maximus* (the highest priestly office) for life, and finally securing a temporally unlimited and nonspecific *imperium* that guaranteed him supreme command of the army as well as ultimate decision-making authority in all foreign affairs and questions concerning the provinces. The summary of his deeds, composed shortly before Augustus's death in 14 AD and inscribed on steles throughout the realm, impressively documented the rhetorical,

27 BC – 284 AD

52 The emperor offering a sacrifice. Augustus had himself portrayed here as a moral example of piety, in keeping with the longstanding republican ideal. Rome, Museo Nazionale delle Terme.

53 The emperor as field general in heroic pose. In closely and subtly interwoven representations, the reliefs of the armored figures announce a new golden age. The central theme is the negotiated return of the battle standards lost by Crassus in a battle with the Parthians. Rome, Vatican Museum.

54 The emperor as citizen: The cameo shows Augustus wearing the citizen's garland granted him by the Senate in 27 BC. This *corona civica* altered quickly from a simple crown of oak leaves into a symbol of monarchic dominance. London, British Museum.

legal, and psychological finesse with which Augustus had officially rescued and rebuilt the Republic, and with what vigor it was at the same time in fact dismantled. When this system—built around a certain charismatic person who in fact had the necessary qualities to make it work (namely, Augustus himself)—devolved upon his death in 14 AD to a successor, Augustus's step-son Tiberius, the Republic became a monarchy in form as well as in fact.

The aristocracy's economic base: Country villas, town houses, and free time

In contrast to the internal conflicts of the 1st century BC, when expropriations, slave uprisings, civil wars, and the burdens of supporting huge armies outside its home borders had struck a heavy blow against the wealthy and had pulled agriculture down into a decline, the long-lasting peace initiated by the regency of Augustus led to rapid prosperity. Four criteria defined who was a wholly acceptable member of the Roman upper class: wealth, higher political or administrative office, social reputation, and membership in an *ordo* (class) such as the senate, the knighthood, or local honorarium (*ordo decuriones*). Aristocratic birth, on the other hand, was no precondition in itself for social standing, therefore The nobility were divided into the *nobiles* and the *homines novi*, the "new men" (like the nouveau riche).

Because one's standing as a Roman aristocrat conferred certain duties as well as many privileges, maintaining that status demanded constant mobility. The base of wealth was the great estates: Less than 6 percent of the population owned more than 90 percent of the farmland in the entire realm. The *latifundia*—a large serf estate—only rarely formed a contiguous property; rather, they were made up of sometimes widely scattered parcels, all of which had to be organized and administered. There were, of course, overseers and qualified persons to manage the estates, but even so, the landowner himself was often required to make inspection tours and to play an active part in his property's administration. And, because official political and administrative business was conducted in the city, the landowners, required at one and the same time to serve their own estates and the Roman government, generally maintained a stately house in the city, and traveled often between their two (or more) homes.

Most often, the actual refuge of the wealthy was a villa near the city—a luxuriously appointed conglomerate of living rooms, bedrooms, gardens, and column-lined halls. These villas were usually built into the side of a hill or some other naturally dominant situation where man-made lines of sight incorporated nature into the inhabitants' world, and where one could both cut a good social figure and fills one's leisure hours. Pliny the Younger, one of the richest Romans at the time of the Emperor Trajan, owned several such villas, one of which—in the upper Tiber valley—he described at length in his letters. What emerges from Pliny's description, augmented by other historical evidence, is the impression that the villa was far more than an architectural structure but the formalization of a lifestyle:

"The villa lies at the foot of a hillock, but looks out over the landscape as if from on high. It faces primarily the south. It is fronted by a large portico which leads to many rooms,

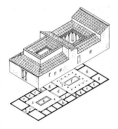

55 City house in Pompeii, reconstruction. The atrium is in the front part of the house, the peristyle court, behind. The other private and public rooms of the house are grouped around these two areas. The fronts of such houses often contained small shops that were only accessible from the street.

27 BC – 284 AD

56 The J. P. Getty Museum in Malibu, CA, built in the 1970s as a replica of the Villa dei Papiri in Herculaneum, which had been buried by Mount Vesuvius in 79 AD. It conveys a good impression of the magnificence and size of the residences of the wealthy built outside the cities.

including an atrium in the ancestral tradition. In front of the hall is a long colonnade with many varied diversions and enclosed with boxwood trees for shade. At the end of the hall, a *triclinium* [dining room] protrudes, and through folding doors one may look out upon meadows and fields. At the other end stands a very large *cubiculum* [bedroom]; under the windows is a *piscina* [pool or artificial pond]—pleasant to the ear and the eye as the water spills down from above and is caught in the basin where it foams. The wide and bright *apodyterium* [dressing room] of the bath leads to a large swimming pool. The rear *triclinium*, with its big windows and double doors, almost allows the grape vines on the slope to grow into the house. Marble seats, each next to a small spring, are placed all around. Everywhere one hears the sound of little watercourses that are conducted through pipes and can be directed by hand; by this means,

57 The villa of the emperor Hadrian, built 130–140 AD near Tivoli, in the vicinity of Rome, was a gigantic architectural conglomerate of structures of various geographical and chronological origins. Model.

one can water first this, then that, garden plot—or all at once. ... These are only some of the reasons why I prefer this villa to my others in Tusculum, Tiburnium, and Praeneste, because here the *otium* [leisure] is more profound, more fruitful, and more certain: no pressure to put on a toga, and no invitations from anyone."
(Pliny, *Epistulae* 5, 6, 14–46).

Politics, mythos, and art: Artistic media as the organ of ideology

"Official" Roman art certainly had a strong political and ideological component, a characteristic that with the passing of

time and the millennia-long accretion of humanistic values has lessened appreciation of the
Romans' works. Scholars and critics have tended
to regard Roman art as merely functional and
"profane," something that borders on the level of
banal commercial art, especially in contrast with
the supposedly nonutilitarian, free, and inspired
art of the Greeks. Such judgment, however,
misses the target. For one thing, no art in any
society, whether ancient or modern, is apolitical.
Every work is a product, and thereby also a
mirror of social conditions, however they may
appear to be filtered or manipulated by the
conscious or unconscious intentions of the artist.
What is so clear from the political and ideological implications of Roman art, and what gives
the dogmatic aspects of Roman art such sali-
ence, is its relatively simple structure: Roman art
is, if you will, art produced under contract within
a centrally and hierarchically organized environment, as opposed to a product of a pluralistic social system with great range for give and
take.

The "golden age" proclaimed by Augustus—
equated by the ruling classes in every sense
with the pinnacle of the Roman Republic, though
it was in fact the slick transfiguration of a putsch
and the establishment of a monarchy—served as
the ideal in all the media of the period. In the
poetry or prose of Horace, Virgil, and Ovid, in
private and public art, architecture, festivals,
and sacrifices—Augustus and his reign enjoyed
a regular mythical inflation. With refined com-
positions, pictures presented the theme of the
golden age in constantly new variations. For
example, in the Tellus Relief of the Ara Pacis
(**64**), the peace altar that Augustus erected in
Rome, the richly suggestive formal language
displays in eternal, classical equanimity an
allegorically bucolic scene in which the ideology

58 The Vienna Augustus
cameo. Above: Augustus as
Jupiter within the circle of
Roman gods and his family.
Below: After a battle victory,
a *tropaion* is built and
prisoners made into slaves.
Vienna, Art History Museum.

27 BC – 284 AD

59 Even if the exact meaning of the illustration of the
Portland vase is not known,
clearly its general theme has
to do with the world of the
upper class. In 1786, Josiah
Wedgewood completed a
model from which many
contemporary copies were
made.

49

More than Money: Roman Coins

60 Heavy Roman money with the image of a bull, ca. 280 BC. Berlin, State Museum.

Like the beginnings of the Roman Republic itself, the origins of Roman coinage remain in the dark. The oft-quoted report on the system of coinage and its history in the *naturalis historia* of Pliny the Elder (Book 33, chapters 42–44) is hardly reliable. The use of money as an economic standard of exchange appeared relatively late in Roman civilization; when it did emerge, it replaced an older system based on livestock trading, first with gold and later with minted coins. Tellingly, the Roman word *pecunia* ("money," "wealth") derives from *pecus* ("cattle," "livestock"), a connection that was directly visible in the figure of a cow that appeared on the first gold mintings, and which the Romans recalled even centuries later when a system of various denominations of coined money had been firmly established.

As the empire expanded, the Romans fused their own autonomous money system with the conventions of the Hellenistic Greek world. Early on, Roman coins had a unique quality beyond their money value: Coins in Rome were a preferred medium for transmitting pictures and messages. Minted in series, newly released coins could reach the general population very quickly. This made them an ideal medium for spreading political messages as well as for the state to disseminate its self-image.

Roman coins were decorated with diverse pictogram-like scenes that made appeals to the citizenry (for example, two hands grasping each other as a symbol of *concordia*) or referred to the strength and power of the state (the prow of a ship to symbolize the navy, memorials of captured weapons or images of the goddess Victoria as symbols for military success). Images of *pietas*, the central Roman virtue of religious piety, drew upon pictures of gods and heroes as well as upon processions and religious or cult rituals. Coins were sometimes inscribed with slogans related to the pictorial theme or with the signatures of the *tresviri*

More than Money: Roman Coins

monetales, the elected minting officials.

During the civil wars of the 1st century BC, the complex pictorial symbolism of the coins shifted toward more topical images of personal propaganda, drawing heavily on current events. The coins thus bear witness to the inner conflicts and disunity of the state. Political portraits turn up with equal frequency as the first visual representations of the alleged genealogy of individual families drawing on the state mythos. Julius Caesar, for example, claimed that the goddess Venus was the mother of his clan, the *gens Julia*; shortly before his assassination in 44 BC, he even minted his own image with the inscription *dictator perpetuo* ("dictator for life")—a huge insult to all the traditional pluralistic and consensual political traditions of the Republic. The coins of the imperial period were stereotypic and graphic. Normally, one side bore a portrait of the emperor while the back, in codified abbreviations,

61 Golden medallion of Constantius I with an almost pictographic illustration of the conquest of London in 296 AD. Berlin, State Museum, Coin Cabinet.

sported symbols and personifications of virtues, images of the gods, or religious scenes to serve as propaganda or expound upon imperial policy (**61**). With the growing dominance of the military, minted messages to the soldierly public also proliferated. Only the more valuable coins made of precious metals showed relief-like scenes with more complex motifs, references to the military victories of Rome, or an individual emperor's vision of state or religion.

62 Emperor Septimius Severus (193–211 AD) used almost every possible pictorial medium to propagandize his establishment of a new ruling dynasty through depictions of family members. London, British Museum.

63 Band relief of Trajan's Column in Rome shows scenes from the war campaigns against the Dacians. Especially emphasized is the army's engineering skill; here, the army is shown building a field camp.

64 Tellus relief from the Altar of Peace in Rome, dedicated in 9 BC.

of prosperity and the mythology of statism are smelted into a metaphor of the ideal society. The altar itself, adorned with many other, similar pictures, was incorporated into a gigantic sundial, which itself bore many references to the important dates in Augustus's life as well as his political and military careers. It is a dynamic monument complex in which Augustus is finally shown as the perfection of all creation. Similar fusions of myth and political ideology are also found in art works stemming from private life, whether from the immediate circle of the imperial court, such as the famous Vienna cameo of Augustus (**58**), or from the world of the wealthy upper class, such as the Portland vase in London (**59**).

As the empire became more firmly established, the structure of its pictorial language was simplified. Richly allusive camouflage could well be dispensed with in the age of Augustus, to be replaced by unalloyed pictorial concepts centered on the emperor or some accessible message. A new genre of picture arose—the "historical relief," which allegorized imperial virtues within an apparently real historical scene. A closer inspection, however, of a relief such as the one on Trajan's Column in Rome reveals that it is not an authentic, documentary-like depiction of the *Dacia* campaign, but rather a synthesis of several different Roman war victories and a demonstration of Roman technological superiority over the culturally inferior enemy who are rendered virtually witless through panic. And in spite of its "photographically" realistic style, the famous *alimentatio* scene on Trajan's Arch in Benevent (**114**) makes no reference to an historical event; it is, rather, a piece of propaganda promoting lordly virtue, in the guise of the fatherly solicitude of the emperor supplying food (*alimentatio*) to the needy.

The scenes on the Arch of Constantine in Rome make it abundantly clear that a stylized repertoire of allegorical pictures developed over the years that served an ideological purpose, even when recycled. Only a few of the reliefs were created especially for the arch; most were borrowed from structures dating from the reigns of Trajan, Hadrian, and Marcus Aurelius. That such images were used on the later monument exemplifies the direct political and ideological references to the past typical of the Constantine understanding of state.

Splendor and luxury of the Roman upper classes

When, in his biography of Augustus, Roman author Suetonius (ca. 70–150 AD) claims that the emperor "beautified Rome to such an extent that he could rightly claim to have found a city of bricks and left a city of marble," he is no doubt exaggerating, and yet there is a kernel of truth in his hyperbole. Buildings were renovated with great energy, and magnificence and luxury became the hall-marks of private villas, residences, and palaces. At first, luxurious architecture and furnishings were limited to public undertakings: In his *res gestae*, the summary of his deeds published at the end of his reign, Augustus

27 BC – 284 AD

65 Rome, Arch of Constantine, 315 AD, south side. The pictures in the round frame date from Hadrian's reign; the large reliefs above come from the era of Marcus Aurelius; those within the passages are from Trajan's forum.

66 The Villa Jovis, built by Tiberius on Capri, is an early example of a luxurious emperor's villa.

27 BC – 284 AD

67 Odysseus and his companions blinding the giant Polyphemus. Statue group from an imperial villa near Sperlonga. Reconstruction.

took credit for beautifying many buildings in Rome out of his own pocket. In his private life, however, Augustus lived with traditional republican modesty; in fact, his house on the Palatine Hill was rather small and, in comparison with the residences of his successors, even spartan.

Under Tiberius, Augustus's stepson and successor, all such republican scruples were dispensed with by both emperor and nobility. From now on, Roman emperors were autocrats with immense wealth at their disposal, and they displayed it publicly in what was often legendary splendor as well as privately in their palaces. In the process, the emperors became the model for the wealthy upper classes, as far as their resources allowed. The most expensive building materials were used in the construction of ever larger palace and villa complexes—not only marble and varieties of colored stone, but also precious metals. Such buildings were fitted with tremendously costly interiors, furniture and tableware from all over the empire, and sophisticated technical achievements such as heating and ventilation. They incorporated (as described earlier by Pliny the Younger), natural scenes, grottos, and caves into living spaces, dramatic lighting effected by window placement in walls and doors, rich mosaics and paintings. These trappings not only became the standard but were counterbalanced by equal luxury in all other areas of consumption—in clothing, jewelry, food, and drink. Extravagance literally became the leitmotif of the Roman upper classes, a brilliance that naturally had an effect on their con-

68 The 1st century AD silver treasure of Boscoreale gives an indication of the luxurious table settings of the Roman upper class. Paris, Louvre.

temporaries. This private luxury was often branded as overdone and decadent, but apparently only by those who were unable to keep pace with the example set by the emperor, for on the whole the upper class strove at least in principle to match the imperial household. Thus, many country villas and town houses were built according to the given style of the time, albeit often on a smaller scale.

Tiberius has been described as stingy but he was in fact only careful with public monies. He built a luxurious villa on Capri; today, its remains, including the "blue grotto" built into the villa, give us some idea of the luxury in which he lived. Also legendary was Nero's "Golden House," an immense, opulently decorated palace complex that he built in the center of Rome after the fire in 64 AD. According to Suetonius, "So extensive was the layout that one colonnade is over two miles long. The palace included a pond surrounded by buildings that resembled cities on a lake shore and a garden area that resembled fields, hills with grape vines, and meadows. Everything was adorned with gold, precious stones, and mother-of-pearl. The dining-room ceilings were made of perforated moveable ivory plates so that flowers could be strewn or perfume sprinkled on the guests from above, and the main dining hall was round with a revolving roof like the heavens, depicting day and night." The palace was torn down after Nero's death, and in its place were built both the Colosseum and park grounds—most likely in a calculated act of restoration to the public of privatized ground by a Flavian emperor who maintained the common touch.

The Emperor Domitian spared no expense building his immense residence; its location on Rome's Palatine Hill, in fact, spawned the use of the word "palace." Domitian's original palace was designed to be the seat of all future Roman emperors (**75**). Domitian reportedly had the Temple of Jupiter on the Capitoline Hill plated with 300 tons of gold, and it is unlikely that his Palatine Hill palace would have been any bit less splendid. The emperor's villa near Castelgandolfo, on what are today the grounds of the pope's summer residence, was probably also just as sumptuous. And the villa of Hadrian at Tivoli in Latium (**57**) was practically an entire world in miniature. Hadrian, who had traveled widely, built a richly appointed architectural conglomerate that unified architectural forms from the entire empire into a picturesque collage.

69 Diocletian's palace in Split imitates a military camp at the beginning of the 4th century AD. It was built for the aging emperor. The entire city center of Split today is contained within what were the palace grounds. 19th-century reconstruction.

Art thieves and copyists: Greek art in a new context

More than anything else—at least from the point of view of Greek-oriented humanism—it was the Romans' unrestrained "borrowing" by robbery and copying that fostered a negative image of Roman culture. After the Roman conquest of Greece, it became fashionable among the Roman upper classes to own Greek art and to display it in the house or garden. It is hardly fair, however, to dismiss or to brand this as typical of Roman culture, because in fact something altogether new was emerging: The personal desire for the "venerable" art of the Greeks among wealthy Romans gave rise to a means of artistic expression in relation to individual monuments and their creators that today underpins our own understanding of the artist and his work. For the archaic and classic Greeks, artistic expression and personal, private voice were irrelevant criteria—statues were a matter of craftsmanship as well as components of public life; they never served private needs.

Aside from the various forms of imitation (see p. 62ff.), there were two ways for a Roman to lay his hands on the coveted Greek art. Effective—though extreme—was robbery in the course of military campaigns and suppressions. Many shrines, market-places, and cemeteries were plundered. Demand was especially strong for the works of the classic sculptors of the 5th and 4th centuries BC— Myron, Polykletes, Phidias, Alkamenes, Praxiteles, Lysippos; in fact, the more their works were sought and acquired by nefarious means, the greater their fame grew. Sections of the *naturalis historia* of

70 The Koren porch of the Erechtheum on the Acropolis, Athens, ca. 410 BC.

27 BC – 284 AD

71 Copies of the Erechtheum Koren in Hadrian's villa near Tivoli, ca. 140 AD. The statues were displayed here as part of a recently assembled collection of classic sculpture from a wide variety of sources.

72 Greek bronze sculpture, ca. 450 BC. Ancient plunder, discovered on a Roman shipwreck near Riace. Reggio/Calabria, Museum.

73 Fragment of a Roman plaster-cast head made from an early 5th-century BC Athenian monument. The cast was in turn used to make more copies. Baiae, Museum.

Pliny the Elder read like a *vademecum* of famous Greek statues and sculptors.

Like prisoners of war and captured weapons, which were paraded in triumph before the masses and put on public display in Rome, Greek art was war booty. For a provincial governor, it became standard procedure to embezzle original pieces within his territory and then to sell them to private buyers in Italy. When Cicero served as pro-secutor against Gaius Verres, who as gover-nor of Sicily had carried the plundering of the province too far, the real drift of the charges against him focused less on the art theft per se, but on its privatization and on the governor's illegal self-aggrandizement; officially, the art belonged to the public—to the Senate and the people of Rome.

The second way to acquire Greek art was less spectacular but far more suitable for the needs of private Roman citizens: the massive production of copies, which made available artwork that was either untransportable, un-available, or for some other reason unable to be brought to Rome. Reproductions, moreover, could be made in any quantity. Entire series of copies produced from 100 BC to 150 AD have survived; they have proven useful for archeologists and students of Greek sculp-ture since the originals from the 5th and 4th centuries BC were mostly unique bronze pieces that either had already disappeared with the ancient world or were smelted into weapons during the Middle Ages.

Armies of copyists flooded the public plazas of Greece. Their copying technique was similar to modern reproduction methods: A cast was made of the original with the help of models, and a copy, most often made of plaster, was produced from the mold; the plaster copy in turn served as a model or pattern, through a meticulous measurement process, for a marble statue. Excavations near Baiae on the Gulf of Naples have yielded many plaster casts of such statues. For very large masterpieces, such as the 39-foot-high Athena Parthenos sculpted by Phidias for the Parthenon around 440 BC, copies were made either by hand chisel on the spot in smaller versions, or in full-sized plaster casts of sections, such as those made of the reliefs on Athena's shield. Such copies were abundant throughout the Roman empire and were easily subsumed into the private sphere. Greek art functioned as a kind of showcase collection for the Romans—according to wealth, preference, and taste, thematically organized statuary groups consisting of works of varied origins and periods could be collected.

Culture versus nature: A universal contradiction as social motto

In his *naturalis historia* book 36, Pliny the Elder described the *cloaca maxima*, Rome's largest sewage canal: "The various powers of the waters struggle within, yet the sturdy construction holds them back unrelentingly; falling ruins pelt its arches when there are fires, the ground is shaken by earthquakes, and still the structure remains indestructible after almost 700 years." The warlike vocabulary may seem unusual to us, but Pliny's language is indicative of ancient Rome's fundamental self-understanding: Nature and natural events are things to be overcome, tamed, ruled, and, where necessary, corrected. And as an example of the "correction" of incomplete nature by human hand, Rome's *cloaca maxima* became the archetype for many writers.

"This very Praetor Verres has robbed, stolen, and plundered ancient monuments and artworks, some of which the kings had donated for the beautification of the cities, and others which our generals had given as gifts to the Sicilian cities after their victories. And he did not stop at statues and works of art, but robbed all the temples as well. He did not leave the Sicilians a single god who seemed to him to be relatively skillfully made and from olden times."

Marcus Tullius Cicero, *Against Verres*, 14, in the list of charges against him at his trial in 70 BC

27 BC – 284 AD

74 The Pont du Gard near Nîmes. With a slope of at least 17 inches per mile (i.e., nearly 56 feet every 31 miles), the water conduit spans bridges and tunnels across the hilly terrain.

On the whole, Roman architecture is stamped with the motif of the triumph of civilization over nature. The recurrent theme survives in many permutations in numerous written sources and architectural ruins. In *de aquaeductu*, Frontinus, an official responsible for the water supply of Rome at the time of Augustus (see p. 120ff) compared the perfectly consistent, slight slope of the aqueducts which tunneled through mountains and traversed valleys by means of towering support structures, with the "eternal" Egyptian pyramids. One might say that the two "wonders" of the ancient world differ in that the Roman acqueduct served a practical purpose, though, of course, an ancient Egyptian might say the same about the pyramids. And in the same martial tone as Pliny, Horace, the expositor of Roman glory during the age of Augustus, sang of the bold, cliff-edge Baiaen villas that reached from their rock overhangs almost into the sea as something wrested from the "hostile elements."

Since the Hellenistic period, villas and other prestigious architectural works, as well as streets, bridges, and harbors were no longer considered mere features of the landscape but its focal points. Villas were set on high, wide bases where they appeared to be simultaneously dug into the earth and "nailed" to pedestals that dominated the surrounding terrain. The entire landscape was incorporated into construction plans to provide vistas and sight lines. Roads were pushed through any natural barriers: They crossed valleys, rivers, and swamps by means of ingenious technology (**76**). The building complex of Trajan's Forum in Rome was celebrated for the extensive ground leveling and earth removal necessary for its construction; the height of

75 The palace of Domitian on the Palatine in Rome was built on top of a high support, especially in relation to the depression of the Circus Maximus. Together they remade the Palatine Hill into a single huge edifice. Model. Rome, Museo della Civiltà Romana.

27 BC – 284 AD

the famous pillar indicated how much earth needed to be removed to prepare the construction site.

The drive to master nature is most obvious in the construction of Roman theaters, which was based on a totally different set of principles than those followed by the Greeks. While the main element of the Greek theater was the cavea, or audience area, which was built into a suitably formed natural hillside (the greatest example is the theater at Epidaurus, still standing today), the Roman theater was an upward-projecting, free-standing structure that defied, rather than accommodated, natural irregularities (**92**). The Roman builders did not adjust their structures to suit the environment, they adjusted the environment to suit their plans; they developed methods that rendered the land universally disposable and allowed construction on any site, regardless of natural conditions.

76 The road bridge near Merida, Spain, built during the reign of Augustus, crosses the Guadiana River and its swampy shores in a straight line of several miles' length.

Roman Classicism

The theft and copying of original Greek sculpture were a direct means of appropriating desired works. However, the diffusion of classicism in Roman art was initially less direct but all the more widespread. Roman classicism idealized all the art forms of Greek classicism—not only sculpture but also architecture, painting, ceramics, and more. Roman classicism in the arts drew upon the Greek standards as its own necessary guiding principle. In this context, the adoption of Greek classicism went well beyond the materialistic desire to possess some Greek art objects to decorate one's home or state building or temple which fostered the plundering and copying of Greek originals. Roman classicism, rather, strove for the comprehensive imitation of forms. In short, the classical artists of the 18th and 19th centuries, and subsequent neoclassical movements, were not the first to look back to classical Greece for artistic, aesthetic, formal, and philosophical models.

How, asks archaeologist Paul Zanker, could such a pictorial language consisting almost exclusively of copies, paraphrases, and citations of earlier epochs of art have come to dominate between 100 BC and 200 AD? In an essay titled, "Imitation as Cultural Fate," Zanker finds an answer: When the art of an earlier age comes to be seen as an unsurpassable, perfect ideal, then, at least according to the Roman understanding of culture, "there was no alternative to the constant continuation of imitation, for every departure from the great models would have meant decline." But behind this statement is a critical undertone that asserts that Roman culture lacks originality and independence. Zanker rightly speaks of a "pictorial language" whose vocabulary is derived from Greek art, but this says nothing about the independence or originality of the "text" produced by means of this vocabulary. Rome, thus, was filled not only with statues copied directly from Greek originals, but with

77 Copy of the lost original bust of Doryphoros, made by the famous Greek sculptor Polykleitos, ca. 430 BC. The precisely arranged hair and nonindividualized physiognomy served as a model for the hair of the statues of Augustus (52–54). From Herculaneum. Naples, National Museum.

Roman Classicism

groups of statues that drew upon classical Greek style and form but used their own distinct motifs and served their own social purposes. Such "classic" statues decorated building facades, gardens, and parks; they could be found by the hundreds in theaters and bath houses, and, in their abundance and their function, they demonstrate something new and typically Roman—Greek art turned into decorative and imposing window dressing. Similarly, Greek architecture was copied, imitated, and imported into Roman architecture. Indeed, the principle of the collage of various set-pieces—of an authentic copy, an imitated Greek form, new motifs and arrangements, and independent Roman pictorial or architectural patterns (for these, too, existed)—is the essence of Roman art. This merging of art forms was an entirely constructive tendency within Roman culture, and was somewhat reminiscent of the post modernism movement, demonstrating the ancient roots of our modern understanding of eclecticism.

We may be inclined today to see the rejection of classicism in the 3rd century AD as the turning point toward decline in the Roman empire. In fact, at the beginning of the Late Antiquity, an entirely new pictorial language emerged with a vocabulary that corresponded to the "new texts" necessary

78 Columns and capital from the east side of the Erechtheum on the Athens Acropolis, ca. 410 BC.

within the framework of the changed social situations—a pictorial language whose formalistic, ceremonial stasis would remain in effect well into the Middle Ages, and that suggests anything *but* the downfall of Rome (see p. 113ff.)

79 Building elements from the round temple for Roma and Augustus, 27 BC. The capitals and necks of the pillars imitate the Erechtheum.

48–47 BC Fixed rents set by law on apartments: a cap of 2,000 sesterce per year in Rome and 500 per year outside Rome in face of an average daily income of 3 sesterce

46 BC Calendar reform based on astronomical year of 365 days per year (Julian calendar) introduced

45 BC Center of Rome becomes a "pedestrian zone;" wagon traffic permitted only at night

15 BC Augustus takes control of the minting of gold and silver; Senate retains copper

6 AD After a catastrophic blaze, the fire department of Rome is increased to 7,000 men

50 AD Paul preaches in Corinth

64 AD Rome burns; new laws limit the height of houses and prescribe the minimal width of streets. Nero builds his palace (*domus aurea*) in the center of the city

69 AD Civil war in Rome following confusion in succession to the throne; Capitol burns to the ground

80 AD Dedication of the Colosseum, erected on the grounds of Nero's city palace which had been destroyed in 68

27 BC – 284 AD

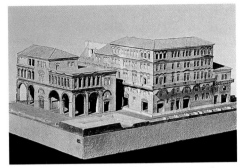

80 Four-story apartment buildings in the harbor city of Ostia near Rome, 2nd century AD. Model.

Big cities and slums:
In the shadow of ancient architecture

Anyone who has visited Pompeii or Herculaneum and admired the many town houses with their generous floor plans, comfortable furnishings, and luxurious decor may find it hard to believe that early big-city living also had its darker side, but this is precisely what the tranquil country towns of Campania suggest. The Roman "suburbs" ("lower city") south of the Quirinal and Viminal Hills were so densely developed with multi-story apartment houses that sunlight could hardly reach into the narrow alleys between them. In the harbor city of Ostia, several such houses are still standing and in good condition.

Day and night, Rome was a loud city. A vast account of impressions of city life in the "suburbs" was compiled by Ludwig Friedländer in 1861 in the German first edition of his *Roman Life and Manners under the Early Empire*:

"Even before daylight, the bakers were hawking their wares and the shepherds their milk. Then the children began to practice the alphabet and to spell in chorus, and hammers and saws were set into motion. Creaking wagons dragged along blocks of stone and tree trunks until the earth shook. Beasts of burden and porters bumped against pedestrians. The air was filled with the unceasing clamor of a procession of priests of Bellona rushing past, by the chattering voice of the shipwreck victim begging for alms, the crying of the cripple, the calling of traders, and the gamboling of clowns. Even at night, the noise did not stop. The rattling of the travel coach that was not allowed to drive in the city during the day disturbed sleep at night. On top of that came the bawling of gangs of roving ruffians and drunkards. Deep in the night, when all the houses were locked and the lights extinguished, then Rome became eerie and dangerous. The many robbers were not the only danger; tiles fell from the roofs, and from upper-story windows toilet pots were emptied, or garbage was tossed out, to land with a crash on the paving stones below."

Just as apartment buildings or rental properties are today bought for investment purposes, they were often objects of financial speculation in ancient Rome as well. In the best of circumstances they might yield high profits, but the common occurrence of fires could just as easily

ca. 100 AD Roman mail service reached its high point: letters travel at an average of 28 miles per day on land

121–125 AD Hadrian tours the provinces

147 AD 900-year anniversary of Rome celebrated with games lasting several weeks

ca. 160 AD Basic wage of a legionnaire is 3 sesterce per day; top racing jockey in Roman Circus earns up to 50,000 sesterce per victory

ca. 200 AD Census reveals 28 public libraries in Rome

27 BC – 284 AD

The satirist Juvenal describes life in the lower city of Rome in the 1st century AD: "Is anyone who lives in cool, high Praeneste or in the simple *suburb* of Gabii afraid of a collapsing house? Our city [Rome] is mostly supported only by thin posts. The only countermeasure found by the administration was to smear clay on the crack, and then to sleep well, even when we live constantly under the threat of collapse. One must also be careful to live where there are no fires. 'Water!' cries a neighbor, dragging his miserable household goods out of the building. Already the smoke is pouring out of the upper story. But you don't notice it when the people from the lower floors have fled, you will be the last to burn if you live directly under the roof. ... However, most people die through lack of sleep—does any city apartment allow sleep? Only the rich are able to buy themselves rest, even in Rome. ... And you must be vigilant about the dangers of the night: you are foolish if you go out to eat without finishing your will, for you will be threatened by death in many forms. Therefore, hope that you will be graced with no more than a chamber pot being emptied on your head."

Juvenal, *Third Satire*, II, 188–310

81 Rental apartment building on the Via de Diana in Ostia, 2nd century AD. Reconstruction.

be disastrous for the investor (not to mention the tenants!). Apartment buildings were cheaply built out of tiles, wood, and poured cement, with no heating or sanitation; they quickly fell into disrepair, and from there to slum conditions. Rents were driven as high as possible: The ground floor usually included a shop of some kind facing the street, and above it were one and two-room apartments, some facing the street and others only the lightwell. Unlike today (except in older walkups), the higher the apartment, the lower the rent.

Fire was not the only hazard in these buildings. Construction was so poor and so cheap that they were also vulnerable to collapse. Thin walls, false ceilings and floors, minimal space between houses because of the cost of land, and the tendency to build taller and taller houses to optimize on the rental potential of a given piece of land—all these factors, after the great fire during the reign of Nero, prompted a series of building regulations that established a maximum building height (at first 95 feet, or 6–7 stories; later 57 feet, or 5–6 stories), and a minimum width for streets (approximately 19 feet). These were social achievements typical of the popular regency of Nero, but they did little to alleviate the problems of mountains of garbage, infestations of rats, and cholera and plague epidemics that afflicted the residents of the dense urban settlements.

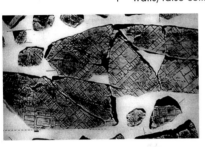

82 Layouts of apartment houses in the "suburbs" of Rome on fragments of the ancient marble city map documenting the shape of the city at the time of the emperor Septimius Severus at the beginning of the 3rd century AD. The map was affixed to the Nerva Forum in Rome.

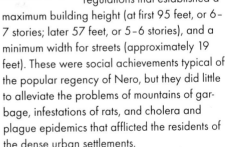

Roman recreation

Perhaps no other aspect of old Roman culture seems so familiar to the people in western countries who have had some exposure to literature or popular media than the excesses of ancient Roman pastimes. However, probably no other aspect of Roman life is so misunderstood today as the games in the circus and arena, the theater and the baths. One thinks with a titillating shudder of the slaughtered gladiators and spectacularly fatal accidents at the chariot races—all metaphors for the bloody face of ancient Rome as delivered to us by historical paintings of the 17th and 18th centuries, by 19th-century dramas, and finally by blockbuster movies like *Spartacus* and *Ben Hur*. What few realize is that the bloody circus and arena games had already aroused criticism in ancient Rome, but it was the moralizing Christian view that used these excesses to damn a whole culture.

The reality is more complicated. Roman theater grew out of rural folk festivals and rituals. Because of its potentially revolutionary content and the masses of people drawn to it, for a long time the ruling authorities remained wary of theater and responded with a plethora of regulations. For example, until late in the Republic, both the stages and the tiered seats for the audience could only be built of wood, required special construction permission, and had to be dismantled immediately after the performances. Only around 50 BC, after long debate initiated by Pompey, was the first stone—that is, permanent—theater erected in Rome. In the days of the empire, the Roman theater lost its volatility and became the site of elevated entertainment for performances by contemporary authors/poets as well as for the performance of Greek classics.

The circus games were always a component of the prestige of the state. The drawn-out rect-

83 Rioting in the amphitheater of Pompeii, 59 BC. Drawing adapted from a Pompeian wall painting. Naples, National Museum.

27 BC – 284 AD

84 Pompeian gladiator's parade helmet decorated with mythological scenes. Naples, National Museum.

The Roman House

85 Lower-middle-class apartment buildings in Herculaneum, as they were buried by the eruption of Vesuvius in 79 AD.

Multi-story buildings like those in the congested cities of Rome and Ostia were the exception rather than the rule. In most smaller country towns, the surface area was measured off into large quadrants (*insulae*), which were then further divided into what were originally equal-size parcels. The houses built on these lots filled the entire area available and stood directly next to each other, like postwar row houses.

The atrium house appeared in Italy in the 4th century BC. This type of building, normally one story high, was closed toward the outside. In the center was a courtyard—or *atrium*—covered by a gabled roof except for a single central light well. The rooms were clustered around the atrium: rooms for the family, formal reception rooms, bedrooms, dining rooms, kitchen, and as side chambers the *alae*—

86 Casa del Fauno in Pompeii was a luxurious town house. View toward the garden peristyle where the Alexander Mosaic was discovered in 1832.

open niches for worship of the *Lares* or images of ancestors. The back part of the house consisted of a small, unwalled garden, something like a courtyard. The inwardly oriented enclosure of this style of house (**55**) was completed by the architecture on the street side: Left and right of the normally very narrow entrance were stores that opened only to the street, and not to the house. Only when lack of space necessitated it—as in Herculaneum—were such houses built with two stories.

According to the owners' financial resources, this architectural format could be expanded to become a city palace, as in the houses of Pompeii. All that was needed was additional ground within the *insula*—the large, densely occupied tenement block that incorporated multiple dwellings following the same general pattern as the

The Roman House

87 Alexander Mosaic from the Casa del Fauno in Pompeii. 19th-century drawing of the find showing the missing areas and ancient traces of restoration. Naples, National Museum.

domus, the single-family atrium dwelling described above. The small garden could be expanded into a splendid courtyard surrounded by a colonnaded portico called a *peristylium*, after the model of wealthy Hellenistic-Greek houses. The Casa del Fauno, stretching over 6,500 square feet in Pompeii, united two atria and even two large peristyles, one roofed and another laid out as a garden area.

Most often, these houses were oriented to the south, and the rooms were arranged both to avoid the summer heat and to collect the winter sun; elaborate heating arrangements were typical only in regions that did not enjoy the milder Mediterranean climate. The furnishings and decorations of the house depended on what the owner could afford. The houses of Pompeii were filled with plain wooden furniture and simple ornamental wall paintings as well as more elaborate wooden furniture, candelabra and couches made

from various metals, filigree work, detailed wall paintings and floor mosaics, and sculptures decorating the peristyle. Literary reports tell us of expensive cushions, fabrics, ivory trinkets, and more, but actual artifacts are rare because such items tend to decay. Still, despite such suggestions, it is probably mistaken to imagine entire towns or cities of sumptuously appointed homes bulging with furniture and other household equipment. Rather, rooms on the whole were quite spartan; there were in fact only a few types of furniture: a bed or couch for sleeping or resting, a chest and cabinet for storage, and small tables and low stools.

88 An example of luxurious Roman furnishings: an ornamented folding tripod of bronze, 250–300 AD. Malibu, CA, J. P. Getty Museum.

89 The thermal baths of Caracalla, built in Rome between 212 and 217 AD, covered an area of 3,760 x 3,680 feet and consisted not only of the baths themselves but also encompassed generous park grounds. Model.

27 BC – 284 AD

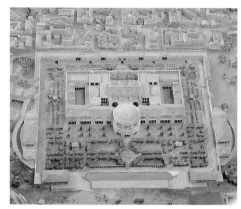

angular architectural form of the arena resembles the Greek hippodrome, but a podium with obelisks divided the race track into two areas. The largest and oldest Roman circus was the Circus Maximus in Rome proper (**75**), which since the 4th century BC had been continually expanded into an enormous complex with room for more than 250,000 people. Public festival games took place here: Around 50 BC, Rome had 109 official holidays, most of which were marked by extravagant presentations in the Circus. Ritual processions and triumphal parades showed off their splendor and the largest animal baitings were also held here. Most popular, however, were the chariot races. The four- or two-horse chariots belonged to wealthy Romans, and successful chariot drivers soon became racetrack stars—the precursors to jockies like Willie Schumaker or race-car drivers like Mario Andretti—on whom vast amounts of money were wagered.

In contrast to the Circus programs, the games in the amphitheater were mostly sponsored by the emperor or by well-to-do public figures at their own cost. Such magnanimity was a guarantee for long-lasting popularity.

The gladiatorial games probably derived from Etruscan burial ceremonies. They were not al-

90 Right: The Naumachie (staged sea battle) presented by the emperor Claudius in 52 AD on Lake Fuccino near Rome. Reconstruction in *Was ist Was*, vol 82, *Gladiatoren* (Nuremberg, Germany: Tessloff Verlag, 1987).

ways struggles to death—though this undoubtedly did sometimes occur. Gladiators were rigorously trained at great expense in special schools; as an investment, Caesar himself maintained a camp with 1,000 gladiators. Not all were slaves; the majority, in fact, were freely employed. Like the chariot drivers (and prize fighters), successful gladiators could achieve fame and wealth if they had negotiated an advantageous division of the prize money with their "owners."

Architecturally, the amphitheater is a Roman invention and was at first, like the theater, a provisional wooden building. The earliest stone structures were built in the late 1st century BC, and by the next century practically every larger city boasted an amphitheater. In Rome, the first stone arena, the Colosseum, was not opened until around 80 AD. Like modern football stadiums, these buildings were often situated at the edge of the city so that riots and upheavals would not take over the city. The compartmentalized building structure with many walls separating audience cells allowed a simple forced evacuation if necessary. Technically, the amphitheaters were works of wonder. Elaborately constructed cloth roofs shaded the audience from the sun, roomy cellars accommodated cages for the animals used in baitings and

The Roman philosopher Seneca wrote in a letter on the annoyances of a visit to the thermal baths:

"On all sides there is confused noise. When the stronger patrons do their exercises and swing their barbells, one must hear their groaning, hissing, and panting. If you run into an idler having a massage, you must hear the slapping of the masseur. Then, if someone is playing ball who cannot play without screaming, it's all over. Take a quarreler, a thief caught in the act, and a singer, and add them to those who are splashing loudly as they jump into the water! And then imagine a hair puller crying out his services until someone has him pull out the hair under his armpits and then starts screaming himself. Finally, there are the purveyors of baked goods and sausages, waiters from the bars."

27 BC – 284 AD

91 Accident at the Circus: Ben Hur (here, Charlton Heston's double) runs over a fallen competitor. Film still from MGM's *Ben Hur* (1959).

27 BC – 284 AD

equipment for moving stage sets; some amphitheaters could even be flooded for the presentation of sea battles.

The Roman baths, with their low admission fees, were very popular. Sometimes, as in the city of Rome, they were given to the city by the emperor. The bath complexes donated by Trajan, Caracalla, or Diocletian were as large as 37 acres in area. Basically, the baths consisted of a regimented series of cold, warm, and sweat baths with a large bathing pool at the center. Elaborate floor and wall heating systems heated both air and water in the sweatrooms to near-sauna levels. The complexes included libraries, parks, and gardens to entertain patrons at their leisure, as well as physicians' practices and facilities for an almost unlimited number of games and sports. The baths also offered less "wholesome" entertainment: Prostitution was ubiquitous, as was gambling and trade in stolen goods.

The Roman leisure culture offered emperors, senators, and well-heeled citizens the ideal opportunity to advertise themselves through patronage and spectacular exhibitionism. Exotic animals were

92 The theater of Aspendos in Turkey was built in the 2nd century AD and is one of the best surviving examples of Roman free-standing architecture.

acquired regardless of cost, the amphitheater was fitted with more and more sophisticated equipment, and bath complexes were decked out with colored marble interiors, expensive statues, and illusionist wall painting that rivaled the luxurious insides of villas and palaces. Behind all this expense and energy devoted to leisure, however, lay the symptoms of a growing

93 The Forum Romanum was not only the political center and formal public showplace of Rome, but, with its bordering basilicas, it was also the economic center. Reconstruction from 1901.

94 The forum in Pompeii, with its long rectangular plaza. A podium temple stands on one of the narrow sides and the magistrates' building on the other. Together with the shrines and market buildings bordering the long arms of the plaza, the arrangement, with its dual function of marketplace and administrative center, is typical of the *fora* of smaller country towns.

(and not unfamiliar) social problem: Entertainment could be a drug, a distraction from the missing substance of life, as well as from unemployment. So, just as the games and races, the baths and theater may loom as precursors to many aspects of modern life—to horse racing and prize fighting, health clubs and luxury spas—so the overall picture of a culture addicted to its own amusement at any cost finds its origins in ancient Rome.

Urban society

The distinguishing feature of a Roman city was its status as *municipium* rather than a settlement. The right to self-administration was an important element of a city charter, and political engagement in the community constituted a central aspect of the life of the upper classes. City offices were voted

27 BC – 284 AD

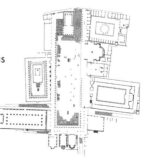

The Family

95 Portrait on a mummy case of a well-to-do Roman from Egypt, ca. 150 AD. Providence, Rhode Island, Museum of Art.

As the foundation stone for the entire state, the Roman family was the smallest unit of the republican constitution. The Law of the Twelve Tables (see p. 31) granted the *pater familias* a special position before the law: He held the power of life and death over his children and slaves. The marriage procedure, which was more like a sale than any other kind of ceremony, put a wife at her husband's disposal body and soul, and all material property lay exclusively under his authority. Despite the rigorous hierarchical order of Roman society, however, there was no rigid separation between a domestic female realm and a public male realm—as was true of ancient Greece. The Roman woman was a personage outside the house and was gladly seen in public. Moreover, the broader Roman concept of family also included the *clientes*; these were free citizens who had bound themselves to a rich lord as retainers; to him they offered their social and political support and in return they received economic and legal protection.

In the 1st century BC, there was a nostalgic trend to harken back to the "good old days." Such complaints always indicate a social shift away from the status quo—that social realities have outstripped certain conservative values. In fact, changes within the structure of the Republic had begun to undermine the *patria potestas*, the principle of paternal power, for the inherent conflict between the clan structure and new economic power was bound to affect the structure of the family. Thus, beginning in the 1st century BC, the position of children and of wives in particular was considerably improved. The woman was allowed some say in the choice of a

96 The Roman family as a community of contract and prestige: The *pater familias*, united with his wife in a handshake, holds the marriage contract in his left hand. The boy's toga signifies his future status as heir and citizen. Tomb relief from Neumagen, ca. 250 AD. Trier, Germany, Landesmuseum.

husband and, more importantly, was granted power of attorney over her dowry; this latter entitlement was no less than a legal capacity to enter into contracts, and would have significant ramifications involving rights of inheritance and the drawing up of a will.

These were important developments indeed, but they are by no means sufficient evidence to suppose that the Roman wife of the 1st century AD enjoyed any degree of emancipation comparable to women's position (in most cultures) today. Divorce and remarriage, as well as civil suits between husband and wife were nothing extraordinary. Anecdotal accounts of women wielding power over their husbands within the households of the emperors and some senators' families are most certainly exceptions rather than the rule; moreover, such historical anecdotes are subject to doubt because they often survive in somewhat biased or mythologized accounts that could just as easily serve misogynistic as feminist ideologies. The actual lack of equality between men and women is demonstrated by the repeated demands for equal legal and de facto status that fill the written records of the imperial period.

With the changed relationships between husband and wife, touted time and again by ancient conservative writers as the herald of decay and the rejection of the "good old

97 Husband and wife as business partners: The Pompeian baker Terentius Neo and his wife, who keeps the books. Wall painting from Pompeii. Naples, National Museum.

ways," domestic life also changed. The woman's field of action expanded, and some Roman marriages were not only partnerships for life but for business in which the wife and husband shared equal responsibility. It was no longer just men who might take a slave or other (often married) woman as a lover—in the course of time, such arrangements became available to women too, even if they were not common practice. Unlike the pre-Christian centuries when the supply of slaves almost outstripped demand, slaves in the Roman empire at some point ceased to be regarded as perpetually dispensable commodities but became an integral part of the household. Similarly, children were no longer simply regarded as the property of the lord of the house, subject to his moods for better or worse, but were given some freedom to develop into their own persons.

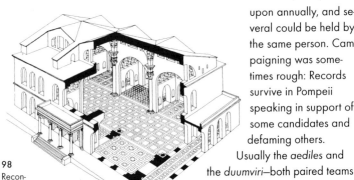

98
Reconstruction of the
Basilica Nova in the
Forum Romanum: Like the
other basilicas lining the
Forum, the gigantic building,
begun by the emperor
Maxentius in 306 AD and
completed by Constantine in
330, served for trade, public
speeches, and court
proceedings.

27 BC – 284 AD

upon annually, and several could be held by the same person. Campaigning was sometimes rough: Records survive in Pompeii speaking in support of some candidates and defaming others.

Usually the *aediles* and the *duumviri*—both paired teams of officials filling a single office jointly—were elected as individuals, rather than as ready-made teams. The *duumviri* were a pair of officials who collectively performed the role of a modern mayor of the city. Two-member collegial teams, like the annual elections, were principles that were supposed to prevent the insidious development of tyranny or monarchy, and survived in form into the days of the empire as a relic of the republican constitution. The most important duties of the *duumviri* were the administration of finance and the pronouncement of justice. The *aediles* were concerned with daily business: They saw to street repair, market surveillance, maintenance of temples, fountains and water lines, tax collection, and organization of the police and fire departments, in all of which they were supported by other city officials.

In addition to these elected officials, there were other bureaucratic organizations that were important for the functioning of the city. The *decurion* order consisted of the city's 100 wealthiest families—later felt to be a dubious honor since membership was attended by considerable special communal taxes (see p. 113). Every fifth year a *census* was taken, an income review that served as the basis for the recomposition of the *decuriones*. As a committee, the *decuriones* had considerable influence on city management.

99 Campaign slogan on the wall of a house in Pompeii, 78/79 AD.

In addition, colleges of religious officials and professional organizations also had some influence. The city was zoned into neighborhoods that served their own protective gods and sometimes demanded offerings for them from strangers passing through, an extortionary waylaying of travelers whose booty was distributed among the needy of the district. Finally, the voices of the various priesthoods, as well as societies and associations, also carried weight in the city. In this sense, Roman society was highly organized, and the organizations commanded attention because they often exerted considerable influence on the votes of their members. The *duumvirs* Holconius Priscus and Ceius Secundus, elected in 79 AD in Pompeii, owed their offices to the solid support of such organizations, to which they had promised various favors in return.

Craft, trade, and processing raw materials: The business and labor world between class organization and slavery

The ancient Roman world of business and labor took various forms but was relatively simple in structure. In individual sectors, division of labor tended to be quite limited. Most commercial enterprises and trading houses were small family-owned businesses that rarely employed anyone outside the family. However, in a given location, the sheer number of similarly oriented, interwoven enterprises could lead to something resembling an industrial monoculture—such as the large number of textile concerns in Pompeii. Such concentrations could lead to considerable environmental pressures, about which people complained but nothing changed: Dyeing houses, textile mills, tanneries, and manufacturers of fish sauce, for example, must all have produced a pestilential stink and terrible water pollution in Pompeii. Lime kilns and large pottery

100 Public flush toilets, like these with 20 marble seats in Ostia, belong to the basic equipment of Roman cities and offered particular opportunities for interpersonal communication.

27 BC – 284 AD

101 Bake shop with customers and clerk on a Pompeian fresco. Naples, National Museum.

102 Ancient shop sign of a slaughterhouse. Dresden, Ancient Collection.

103 Bakery in Pompeii with rotating mills and large bake ovens.

104 Shop offering warm food and drink (*thermopolium*) in Pompeii. Such fast-food forerunners, sometimes richly furnished with tables, benches, wall paintings, and marble sheathing, were found on almost every corner of the Vesuvian city.

factories left behind broad areas of deforestation and erosion in their search for fuel; in fact, their activity is one of the major reasons why large portions of the once thickly forested Mediterranean coast are still denuded today.

The structure of the businesses also demonstrates how little division of labor there was—there was almost no distinction between production and trade. Food products such as bread, fruit, and vegetables were sold directly by farmers or manufacturers (such as bakeries) and were not normally transported beyond their originating region. Even in the case of monoculture with supraregional markets, wholesalers or middlemen were rare; rather, individual local sectors were often cooperatively organized and distributed their products themselves. In the Terra Sigillata pottery works in southern Gaul, near the present-day town of La Graufesenque, the large pottery kilns were used in common, and the remains of wholly cooperatively run warehouses and bookkeeping have been excavated. A highly specialized trade developed, particularly as to rare luxury articles. For the risky preliminary financing of individual deliveries, there was even a bank that offered credit and loan arrangements to traders who stood to become very rich with luck, or very poor with misfortune.

In Roman cities, trade and commerce were organized in colleges and associations that offered members not only mutually profitable business, but also sociability, religious practice, representation of political interests, and social insurance; in modern terms, such societies combined elements of medieval guilds, modern business associations, private clubs, religious sects, and trade unions. These colleges and associations sometimes possessed considerable wealth and had their own meeting houses. In the economic crisis of the 3rd century AD (see p. 113ff), this high degree of organization became a disadvantage. For the sake of maintaining the economy and securing tax income, they were turned into state-controlled corporations with mandatory membership from which large payments were demanded. Because it was forbidden to resign, it was also effectively forbidden for a member to move or change professions.

Over the centuries, free wage-earners competed with slave labor in agriculture, commerce, and trade. A day-worker always had to search out new work on short notice and always stood on the edge of the social abyss. Only with the end of imperial expansion in the 2nd century AD did the surplus of labor reverse into a shortage of labor—though this situation was still regulated by the government and forced small tenant farmers in particular into a kind of servitude. For the small farmer, the problem was no longer the constant threat of competing against slave labor, which opened the way to pressure from large landowners, but the legal regulations binding the land and the concomitant radical taxation of the slight profits that remained for subsistence after the contractual tenancy rents had been paid.

The army also played an important role in the economy (see p. 108ff). As long as troops were stationed in the forts near the borders, the military constituted its own economy. Agriculture and food production, the manufacturing of goods for daily use, as well as the building and repair of weapons all took place for the most part in military production centers, augmented

105   The cloth dyeing house of Primus in Pompeii with the characteristic large kettles.

27 BC – 284 AD

106   Wine cellar in Pompeii with large supply barrels dug into the earth.

107 The thin-walled, brick-red Terra Sigillata ceramic vessels were an imitation of noble metal pieces. The relief decoration was cast in special form bowls, enabling production of a series of similar vessels. Arezzo, Archaeological Museum.

27 BC – 284 AD

by trade with the surrounding region. However, in the 3rd century AD, when large mobile contingents were moved from hot spot to hot spot, the military was no longer to be self-supporting and became instead a huge squanderer of resources whose confiscations and dispossessions could cast an entire region into poverty.

The pageantry of the "little man": The self-dramatization of the middle class

The magnificence and luxury of the Roman upper class are archaeologically well documented, not only in their extravagant architecture but also in the statues, jewelry made of precious metals, pottery, cameos, and portraits that fill the museums of the world. But the fact that the less well-to-do citizens of the city consciously tried to imitate the imposing style of the upper crust is also evident in many less spectacular memorials of the time. One outstanding location where we have found evidence of middle-class efforts at demonstrating their status is in the necropolises that stretched along the main roads in from the city gates. Poorly and richly appointed graves lay side by side; what is striking is the extent to which the less-wealthy families patterned themselves after the style of the rich. Grave reliefs imitated those of the wealthy and the architecture of the tombs followed—in smaller format—the more extravagant architecture of the rich. Such avenues of tombs form, all told, an illustration in stone of the social structure of the town.

Many indications of the middle-class imagination can be found in what are often disparagingly called handicrafts, or arts and crafts. In carelessly cut pictures, gems

108 Street of tombs behind the Herculanean city gate of Pompeii.

imitate "great art" or are adorned with magical motifs symbolic of common superstitions; similarly, precious stones were often replaced by glass paste in bourgeois jewelry. The brick-colored, glaze-like Terra Sigillata tableware with decorative reliefwork portraying Roman daily life and popular myths was series-produced in molds; these dishes were daily ware that even the simplest soldier packed along. Series runs of clay lamps with their crude full reliefs formed a complete compendium of erotic wishes and sexual practices—often clothed in mythical scenes and appearing as themes in the wall paintings in at least one room of less-wealthy households. From the conventional perspective of the art historian, such artistry may be considered second or third rate, but to the social historian it provides rich source material about the circumstances of life for a broad class of the people of ancient Rome.

Of poverty and banditry

How a society deals with its poor and its rich has a direct effect on the amount of crime in that society. This truism was always a topic of discussion among the upper classes in ancient Rome. Not only the *plebs urbana* of the city itself but a large segment of the entire population had no income at its disposal. In the midst of an economic framework characterized by such disparity, work and "getting by" were not possible for everyone, especially when the so-called free market had to compete with slave labor. That the poverty resulting from these conditions reached dismal levels we know only from ancient literature, for poverty, the state of *not having anything*, is precisely *not* manifested in archaeological finds.

109   Roman clay lamp, 2nd century AD. The lamp was filled with oil through the hole in the scene containing figures; the burning wick emerged from the spout.

27 BC – 284 AD

Wall Paintings: The Four Pompeian Styles

110   First style of Pompeian wall painting: Side room of the atrium in the House of Sallust in Pompeii, ca. 200 BC.

111   Second style of Pompeian wall painting: Bedroom (*cubiculum*) in the Villa of the Mysteries near Pompeii, ca. 60 BC.

As scientists have worked on excavating and exhuming the cities and villages drowned in lava when Mount Vesuvius erupted in 79 AD, brilliantly colored wall paintings have come to light; similar excavations have yielded equally stunning discoveries in the luxurious town houses and palaces in Rome and throughout the empire. At first these paintings met little enthusiasm among artistically oriented archaeologists; they were regarded as mere handicraft, like ancient wallpaper, deserving less respect as works of art than the supposed masterpieces of Greek painting that have survived in ancient hymnal descriptions, but not in fact.

But the colorfulness and precise execution of the Roman paintings is still impressive today: ochre, blue, black, and especially the Pompeian red (the composition of which still remains a riddle), provide the ground for additional mixed tones. The walls were painted as frescos—that is, the colors were applied to the still-wet plaster, a technique that

demands a sure and swift painter's hand. Archaeologists classify Roman and Pompeian wall paintings into four stylistic levels, all based on Roman architecture; from concrete imitations of building structure to *trompe l'oeil* architectural paintings and ornamental stagelike settings that incorporate narrative scenes.

In the first, or *incrustation*, style, a wall is divided into rectangular quadrants set above a socle, often with painted columns set in front. This style had already appeared in Macedonian tomb chambers of the 4th and 3rd centuries BC, and after around 200 BC in Pompeii.

The second style, which flourished between 80 BC and 10 AD, retained the socle area but set the columns upon it. "Behind" the columns, in illusionistic perspective, were further architectural elements that often corresponded to nothing in reality but emanated from the artist's imagination.

The third style, dating from about 10 AD to the Pompeii earthquake of 63 AD, enhanced the architectonic

Wall Paintings: The Four Pompeian Styles

112 Third style of Pompeian wall painting: Side room of the atrium in the House of Lucretius Fronto, Pompeii, ca. 50 AD.

113 Fourth style of Pompeian wall painting: Living room in the House of Fabius Rufus, Pompeii, ca. 70 AD.

illusion with depictions of houses, seascapes, and garden scenes knowledgeably painted in deep perspective leading the eye toward a vanishing point. In this style, the painted architectonic foreground has the effect of delicate filigree work and often did away with the concrete illustration of socle area. Integrated into this framework were individual pictures with narrative presentations of mythological or bucolic and idyllic themes.

The fourth stylistic development, from 63 AD to the destruction of Pompeii in 79 AD, reduced the architectonic structure to the point of ornamentation. Walls in this style portray scenes with figures moving within the architectural structure and rarely as individual framed pictures.

The catastrophic eruption of Vesuvius in 79 AD put an end to these particular styles as defined by specialists, but Roman wall painting was by no means vanquished. Reduced in scale, wall painting continued in tombs and catacombs (see p. 118ff) and in the provinces.

The Roman architect Vitruvius, a contemporary of Augustus and author of the only surviving extended treatment of architecture from the ancient world, promoted the polemic against the architectonic unreality of the second style:
"The themes that had once been taken from reality are today distorted by absurd taste. One paints the walls with monsters instead of with recognizable things; in place of columns we find channeled reeds, in the place of gables, rolled leaves and branches and candelabra carrying the image of small temples: From the gables bouquets of flowers grow from winding roots; in between, with no rhyme or reason, we may find sitting figures with half-torsos bearing an animal or a human head. None of that exists in reality; none ever has existed. ... But although people notice these errors, they don't find fault with them; they rather take pleasure in them."

Vitruvius, *de architectura libri decem*, VII, 5, 3–4

27 BC – 284 AD

114 Trajan distributing the *alimentatio*, the governmental food distribution system to poor families with many children supported by a complicated taxation mechanism. Trajan's arch in Benevent, 114 AD.

For the propertied, widespread poverty was always a potential personal threat. Indigency fueled crime, the only remaining source of income for those with no resources. But although murder, robbery, theft, and extortion were common in the cities, they were not the worst problem. A much more over-whelming threat was posed by large organized bands that turned parts of entire provinces into unsecured areas, just as pirates did over large stretches of the Mediterranean. For those in power, such attempts at an alter-native economics seriously threatened to undermine law and order. In contrast, those without means saw such activities as their only somewhat secure chance at survival. The battle against criminal gangs and pirates was troublesome and expensive, and the price finally had to be paid by the wealthy via a special tax. In order to suppress the plague of pirates, in 67 BC, Pompey outfitted 500 ships and put 125,000 men at arms; by so doing, he managed to fulfill his mission within three months. However, the fact that Pompey declined to punish the vanquished pirates with draconian measures—some were actually granted land and helped to settle with considerable state assistance—demonstrates the Romans' awareness that they were dealing with an overarching social, economic, and political problem, not with "simple" criminals.

Preventive measures were actually more expensive than simple punishment. For this reason, ancient Rome only sporadically exercised a kind of social policy according to the engagement of the local administration, or the emperor in power. Though there were many large-scale programs that provided food to the needy by an act of state, we must not jump to the conclusion that the state was being particularly beneficent at such moments. The government was usually able to pass certain measures that, through a complicated taxation process, put the burden of such expense on the wealthy. For just such reasons, the nobility tended to be very critical of socially and politically active emperors such as Nero, and this negative image was perpetuated in the works of ancient writers like Suetonius and Cassius Dio.

Medicine and pharmacology

Our awareness of the highly specialized level of Roman medicine comes not only from the detailed books on the art of healing written by Celsus around 30 AD, or from the writings of the physician Galen from the 2nd century AD, but also from medical equipment uncovered in many excavations. Various medical spatula, probes, pincettes, forceps, needles, saws, bone chisels, knives, scalpels, cupping glasses for blood-letting, and surgical clips suggest that, until well into the 19th century, the medical arts hardly pro-

115 Poverty reconstructed: The food supply for three days and the modest day's ration of the simple soldier—in total, food for four days.

27 BC – 284 AD

116 Street beggars in a Roman city. 19th-century drawing based on a wall painting from Herculaneum.

gressed beyond the limits of the Romans' knowledge.

Physicians were trained in special schools and offered their "arts" either in ambulatory or in stationary practices; the latter might consist of treatment rooms within their own homes or could be a rented room in a public building such as a bath house or a basilica. There were a number of areas of special-ization; we have evidence that there were gynecologists, dentists, eye doctors, and surgeons, as well as more hardened prac-titioners such as military doctors who were notorious for their impatience with protracted healing processes and often opted for imme-diate amputation.

Pharmacology was also quite highly devel-oped. Tinctures, salves, and powders were mixed from a wide variety of ingredients, and the recipes were set down in books. In the legionary camp at the German city of Neuss, which was destroyed in 69/79 AD, remains of the apothecary have survived: traces of cen-taury, thyme,

117 Located on the Gulf of Naples, Baiae was the most important health spa in the ancient Roman empire.

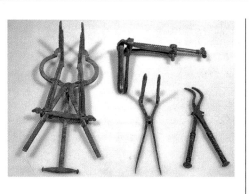

118 Medical instruments from the Surgeon's House in Pompeii. Naples, National Museum.

Saint John's wort, and ironwort were found in the ruins of the camp. It was often difficult to acquire high-quality raw products for medicines; commercially traded products had a shoddy reputation because their high prices tempted producers and traders to stretch the medicine with additives, or even to falsify it entirely. Thus, Pliny describes in the 34th Book of his *naturalis historia*: "The physicians are now far removed from the medicine making that was once the essence of the profession. As often as they now mix something together out of books and then want to test it out on the unfortunate patient, they blindly trust the swindlers who counterfeit the substances."

Based on the Greek practice of cures, the Roman health cure programs were highly developed. Not only individual medical schools, but entire cities and regions (for example, the island of Kos or the Amphiareion near Oropos, north of Athens) advertised for customers and promised a comfortable healing process during a pleasant stay. There are many records of rich customers who treated themselves to such medically justified vacations.

27 BC – 284 AD

119 Sutures, needles, spatula probes, and trepanning saws. Finds from 3rd and 2nd century BC Roman tombs. Excavator's original drawing, 1913.

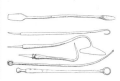

242 BC	Sicily (39)
227 BC	Sardinia (14)
197 BC	Spain (Hispania [10] and [11])
148 BC	Macedonia (21)
146 BC	Africa (38)
129 BC	Asia (25)
121 BC	Gallia Narbonensis (12)
102 BC	Cilicia (29)
81 BC	Gallia cisalpina
74 BC	Cyrene (37)
64 BC	Crete
63 BC	Pontus (24), Syria (30)
58 BC	Cyprus (33)
46 BC	Numidia (Africa Nova) (40)
30 BC	Egypt (36)
25 BC	Galatia (26)
16 BC	Aquitania (6), Lugdunensis (2), Belgica (3)
15 BC	Noricum (8), Raetia (7)
10 AD	Pannonia (16)
17 AD	Cappadocia (27)
42 AD	Mauretania (41)
43 AD	Britannia (1)
46 AD	Thrace (22)
72 AD	Judea (34)
86 AD	Moesia, superior and inferior (29)
90 AD	Germania, superior (4) and inferior (5)
106 AD	Arabia (35)
107 AD	Dacia (17)
114 AD	Armenia (28)
115 AD	Assyria (31)

(Numbers in parentheses refer to the map below.)

27 BC – 284 AD

The creation and administration of the empire

With the incorporation of Dacia into the empire and the establishment of the provinces of Armenia, Mesopotamia, and Assyria during the reign of Trajan, the Roman Empire covered as much territory as it would ever encompass. Since the 3rd century BC, all of the lands beyond Italy that had been incorporated into the empire were organized geographically into fixed provinces (see p. 37). Until Trajan's campaigns once more changed the shape of the empire, the pillars of Roman expansion had been formed by Caesar's Gallic wars, the conquest of Egypt, the German lands and areas on the Danube in the time of Augustus, and the British campaign of Claudius.

At first, the provinces were the sole responsibility of the Senate. By legal statute, the *lex provincialis*, the provinces were administered at the local level by periodically appointed governors and, as subjects of the emperor, paid taxes to Rome. Until 212 AD, citizens in the provinces enjoyed only second-class status relative to the Italians, although the inhabitants of a *colonia* enjoyed a specific city right that offered more than the privileges of a *municipium*.

The legal standing of the provinces was revised a number of times during the centuries, as were their classification and boundaries. In 27 BC, the empire was divided into imperial and

120 The Roman world and its regions during Trajan's reign.

senatorial provinces. The latter consisted of the traditional core of the empire in Greece, Asia Minor, southern Gaul, and northern Africa. No troops were stationed there, and they were ruled by a *proconsul* who was replaced annually. By contrast, the imperial provinces on the edges of the empire were a field for military activity and stood under direct imperial control through the emperor's emissary, a *legatus*. Regardless of a province's senatorial or imperial status, taxes were in all cases collected by a special financial procurator.

This administrative system was radically changed by reforms undertaken by the emperor Diocletian in response to the comprehensive crisis besetting the Roman Empire at the end of the 3rd century AD (see p. 107ff). The Diocletian innovation of the tetrarchy—the simultaneous rule of a college of four allied emperors—led to the creation of four jurisdictional zones (along with three additional capitals—Milan, Trier, and Thessalonica)—in other words, to a decentralization that was favorable to neither Rome nor Italy. Meanwhile, for the sake of more efficient tax collection, the empire was more tightly organized: At first twelve, later fourteen, larger areas called dioceses were formed as superior administrative units. The erstwhile 50 provinces were re-divided into 95 and again, under Constantine, into 117 smaller districts under diocesan control. This system allowed—certainly not for the comfort of the population—the administration to stretch its tentacles into even the most remote villages and created the structure whose byzantine organization, with its ever smaller divisions into subdistricts, lasted well into the Middle Ages.

The non-Roman areas located just beyond the border provinces always

121 The Column of Trajan in Rome. Built as a grave monument, the spirally ascending band relief depicts the successful Dacian wars that led to the incorporation of Dacia as a Roman province.

27 BC – 284 AD

122 The plundering of Jerusalem in 70 AD by the troops of Titus was illustrated as a historical event by such impressive booty as this seven-armed candelabra. Passageway relief in the Arch of Titus in Rome, Forum Romanum.

posed an important question for both state and administration. In the east in particular, these regions had a long tradition of independence and on several occasions involved Rome in complicated wars. Rome pursued a policy of alliance-making that in some cases turned the regions into something like clients of Rome, that is, into economically and militarily dependent vassals who not only adopted the Roman system of administration but almost became provinces. Examples include Cappadocia and Mauretania, which had begun to be treated administratively as provinces in the 1st century BC, and Armenia and Mesopotamia, which for the same reason functioned as loyal allies of Rome until the 2nd century AD.

The *limes* and its *castella*

The northern expansion that began with Caesar's campaigns continued under Augustus. The provinces of Raetia and Noricum, established in 15 BC, were the first firmly established extensions of the empire north of the Alps. Military attacks continued to the north, always pushing further into the Germanic region which at first could only be held by a provisional chain of forts (*castella*) on the Rhine and Lippe rivers. The rather discouraging expeditions of Tiberius as far as the Weser and Elbe, together with the Germani's slaughter of the army of Varus in 9 AD, soundly ended this phase of expansion. From this point on, the empire's northern border had to be defended at all times. The danger posed by the unpredictable Germanic tribes was constant, and its

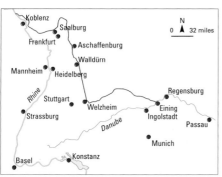

123 The *limes* along the Rhine and Danube, 2nd century AD.

devastating effects—as in the revolt of the Batavians in 69–70 AD or the wars with the Chatti in 83 AD—can be read in excavations of Roman forts with their several feet thick layer of ashes and ruins.

The *limes*—a network of military roads with posts and signal towers—as an extensive border security system grew directly out of a need for defense. It was at first supposed to put a lasting end to the countless German attacks in the conquered territory. For more than two hundred years, the defensive line remained under construction; its traces have been found throughout the empire, but especially in areas where the boundary between the Roman area and the "foreign" territory was not easy to defend—such as along broad riverbeds or steep mountain ridges. The best preserved are the *limes* between the Rhine and the Danube, built in 90 AD to secure the province of Germania; the Clyde-Forth line (Antoninus Pius Wall) in Scotland, and the Solway-Tyne *limes*, better known as Hadrian's Wall, in England. There are also well-preserved sections of the Danube *limes* in Austria, Bulgaria, and Romania. On the other hand, the *limes* that had once stretched straight through the northern Sahara or along the eastern borders of the empire are hardly extant today. The approximately 310-mile-long upper Germanic and Raetian *limes* ran from Hönningen on the Rhine directly eastward through the Westerwald, the Taunus hills, and the Wetterau, then bent sharply to the south by Arnsburg, turning again to the east after about 125 miles by Lorch, near Stuttgart, and continued a further 95 miles to meet the Danube by Kehlheim. An older part of the north-south line ran further westward, from around Aschaffenburg to Heilbronn on the Neckar river (in Germany). Under Trajan, the *limes* was still a

124 Watchtower with a defensive wall and earthen rampart on the Raetian *limes*. Reconstruction.

27 BC – 284 AD

125 Rome in the German forest: The 19th-century Wilhelmine reconstruction of the Roman fort Saalburg near Frankfurt shows a typical auxiliary fort situated next to the *limes*.

In a 1996 "report" on the Germanic tribes, the German magazine *Der Spiegel* heaped one cliché on top of another: "Rome drew off from the restless barbarians, entrenched itself behind the Rhine, the Danube, and the *limes*, and left the intransigent herbivores to themselves. The Germans remained thenceforth in this condition of agony ... For about 300 years the *limes* stood fast as a bulwark against the poorhouse of Europe. Then Rome's strength slackened under the onslaught of the furious plunderers." (Number 44, p. 212)

126 The extreme northern reaches of the empire: Winter along Hadrian's Wall in England.

more or less open territorial division secured by a chain of watchtowers set within sighting distance of each other and a series of forts set back a bit into the interior. Only under Hadrian and Antoninus Pius was the border reinforced by trenches, which allowed few crossings, as well as by palisades and even high walls built up ever higher over the decades and reinforced with stone—in all, a tremendous undertaking.

The first watchtowers on the border were made of wood; later they were made of stone. Depending on the terrain, they were between 13 and 26 feet high and from 1,600 feet to 3 miles apart. The arrow-straight segment of the *limes* between Walldürn and Welzheim was relatively easy to defend, but the rough topography of the Westerwald and the Taunus by the German city of Frankfurt am Main required a denser network of posts. Every tower was armed and stocked with easily ignitable piles of wood or balls of straw that served as a simple but effective warning system. Somewhat behind the line, laid out along well-built roads at intervals of 6 to 20 miles, was a chain of smaller forts for auxiliary troops, that is, for the non-Roman support troops whose number might reach 500 soldiers per fort. The reconstructed Saalburg by Frankfurt (see p. 147) was one such auxiliary fort, and offers us a good glimpse into the daily life in a *castellum*. Spaced at a much greater distance from each other, and sometimes far behind the *limes*, were the legionary camps, the true garrison posts of the army. Normally one, but sometimes two, legions (6,000 or 12,000 men) were stationed in the camps. Along a well developed network of roads and paths, the troops could quickly reach a threatened location without exposing their camp to immediate danger.

The "urbanization" of the military camps: The creation of new provincial centers

The "Romanizing" of a region has always been considered synonymous with the transplantation of culture and a civilized life style into a barbarian diaspora. "The Romans" are supposed to have introduced architecture and sculpture, poetry, street and bridge building, ship travel, wine making, and superior agriculture into a territory inhabited by half-wild tribes. Such was the state of things according to Caesar's *bellum gallicum* (Gallic Wars) or Tacitus's *Germania*—and to many modern authors caught up in the Roman mythos.

But what was this "Romanizing" in fact? At heart, it was war and conquest. Between the reigns of Caesar and Augustus, vast areas of Gaul and Germania were violently "integrated" into the Roman empire. Many camps and forts, originally just provisional military camps with no permanent structures, were built at strategically secure points; gradually, however, these sites solidified into city-like entities. On the west bank of the Rhine in Germany and the Netherlands, as well as along the south bank of the Danube flowing through Germany, Austria, Hungary, and Bulgaria, these military camps were the seeds of far-flung Roman settlements. Nijmegen, Xanten, Cologne, and Neuss, Remagen, Bonn, Mainz, Trier, Regensburg, Budapest—all these cities trace their roots back to large Roman legionary camps.

Colonia Ulpia Traiana
Roman aqueduct
Xanten
RHINE
Castra Vetera I
Castra Vetera II

127 From military camp to city: Colony Ulpia Traiana, near Xanten, Germany, was established in 100 AD as a newly planned veterans' colony, and in the process probably swallowed up the existing temporary settlement next to the military camp, Vetera I, which had been established in 5 BC.

27 BC – 284 AD

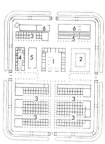

128 Layout of the Lower Bavarian auxiliary fort Künzig, built ca. 90 AD.
1 = *principia* (staff buildings)
2 = *praetorium* (commander's house)
3 = *centuriae* (troop quarters)
4 = *valetudinarium* (hospital)
5 = *horrea* (supply depot)
6 = *stabulae* (stalls).

The process of becoming a city was similar in all cases. Whenever strategic military considerations prompted the Roman authorities to build a permanent base on the site of what had been a pitched camp, the original tent city was replaced first with structures of wood, and later with buildings of stone. Fortifications were improved and the general infrastructure was integrated into the "city" plan. Sources of raw material were exploited, streets were built, and either wells were dug or water was piped in from nearby springs. Since military camps initially had to be fairly self-sufficient, agriculture and manufacturing had to be

129 The northeast Gate of Volubilis (Morocco). In the 1st–3rd centuries AD, at a safe distance behind the *limes*, many cities blossomed. Their impressive ruins are still partly visible today in the Sahara (whose climate was in those days more favorable).

27 BC – 284 AD

developed. Meanwhile, those people who sought the commerce of such a developing infrastructure settled around the camp, either to buy manufactured goods from the camp or to offer their wares or services (like prostitution or gambling). Every legion attracted such a train of civilians, who soon began to mix with the local populations. In time, from the rather provisional chaos of booths and shacks, a permanent settlement arose, often crowned in a formal act of foundation in which the wooden buildings were torn down and replaced with a regularly laid-out settlement. A settlement resembled a military camp in its rectangular organization and included all necessary public buildings and arrangements, such as a forum or a capitol temple. Markets formed, pulling in the surrounding area, and commerce and trade spread out beyond the military base.

130 The Roman city of Augusta Raurica (today Augst, near Basel, Switzerland) developed in 44 BC out of a nearby legionary camp. Model of the city center as it looked in the 2nd century AD.

Together with the military center, the surrounding villages of cabins and shacks, the *canabae legiones*, could develop within a few years into a settlement core that often acquired the rights of a city. The inhabitants of such a city gradually assumed a Roman character. Sometimes the legionary camps were laid out near existent, conquered native settlements. In Germany and the Netherlands, these processes can be traced not only through historical records but through archaeological discoveries as well. From the legionary camp Vetera, built on a slight rise over the confluence of the Rhine and Lippe rivers in 5 BC, a settlement (**127**) had developed that around 100 AD was transformed into a drawing-board city, Colonia Ulpia Traiana; it was granted the highest form of city right. The legal designation *colonia* was also granted to the city of Cologne (Colonia Claudia Ara Agrippinensium), which had developed around 50 AD from the military camp near an old settlement of the Ubian tribe. The city had become an extremely important center of commerce because of the bridge across the Rhine that was secured by the Roman fort near Deutz on the other side of the river.

27 BC – 284 AD

Roman Building Technology

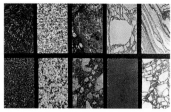

131 A selection of colorful stones typically used in ancient Rome to cover buildings made of poured cement.

Of all the legacies of ancient Rome, none has been more highly respected by the medieval and modern worlds than the engineering achievements of Roman architecture. Not only the size and magnificence of the buildings but their "eternal" durability, together with their symbolic character as ruins, have embued Roman antiquity with a romantic air, still evident today in the landscapes

132 Relief from the tomb marker of the *Haterians* in Rome shows a large crane with which stone blocks were moved by means of pulleys.

of a Piranesi or Canaletto (see p. 134).

Where most ancient Greek architecture consisted of unpretentious and impermanent wood and mud brick construction (the impression that it was characterized by monumental stone and pillar architecture is merely due to the fact that those relatively few edifices survived the millennia, while the more common buildings disappeared in time), the Roman inventions of poured cement and baked bricks revolutionized not only the building forms, but also all the technical, organizational, and social aspects of construction. Like cement today, the Roman *opus caementicium* could be made fluid and therefore could be formed inside wooden sheathing. The cement hardened quickly, could bear almost any weight, and was nearly indestructible. Its unsightly gray color could be decoratively disguised with various kinds of tiling, with polished marble or Travertine slabs. This cement technology, as well as the Roman use of walls of baked bricks, opened up a world of architectonic forms. Façades could be broken by niches, often filled with reliefs, mosaics, or sculptures; rooms could be roofed with poured wide barred vaults or by domes as large as 143 feet in diameter, as in the Pantheon in Rome; support pillars allowed the construction of massive foundations for structures built into hillsides, or

Roman Building Technology

133 Using wooden forms to set up the core of a poured wall. Reconstruction.

for valley-spanning aqueducts and bridges. There really is no way to overemphasize the expanded range of architectural forms facilitated by the basic technology of poured cement and baked bricks.

The Roman era also revolutionized social aspects of building. Whereas Greek cut stone and pillar architecture required many highly specialized manual skills, as well as equipment and labor for cutting, transporting, and installing the heavy building elements, Rome's new technology meant that a large building could be erected quickly. While the process naturally called for supervisors to organize and specialists to plan the work, espe-

cially for wooden construction, most of the labor could be handled by unskilled workers. Thus, slave labor could be broadly used in building, and unskilled day laborers could be hired for transportation and production of cement and baked bricks and for wood preparation. Indeed, this was often the labor structure in the construction industry of the Roman imperial days—it was a kind of job creation program.

Most Roman buildings, however, were not made of stone, although

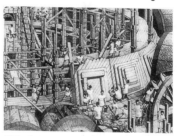

134 Constructing a Roman dome of poured cement over a wooden shell.

the use of stone was always an important symbol of a high culture. Architects were also by no means the only ones involved in the key functions of construction. Rome was well known for its advanced carpentry (*materiatio*) and its well-respected engineering, both of which were especially significant in the military context: The building of bridges and siege machinery and the development of stronger fortifications, palisades, and trenches were central duties of the Roman master builder.

135 Cement kernel covered by tuff and tiles in Pompeii.

136 View of the excavation of one of the Roman ships found on the banks of the Main River near Mainz, Germany; discovered in 1981–82.

Commercial traffic in the Roman empire

With the imperial expansion of the 2nd and 3rd centuries AD, the exchange of wares grew more and more important. Italy was at first literally flooded with imports from the provinces. These imports were not only luxury items but also everyday goods brought in in ever greater numbers by business-minded traders, creating a climate of competition that often proved ruinous for the domestic economy (see p. 38ff). With the empire's continued expansion, however, these commercial structures underwent a radical change. Because of limited capacity, long-distance transportation inflated the prices of imported goods. Shipping was by far the cheapest form of hauling, with each ship able to carry several tons of goods. Every halfway navigable watercourse was used—not only the ocean, but also lakes and rivers. Cities at a distance from the waterways were sometimes connected by a network of canals, so that even inland areas could use a harbor, as archaeologists are often surprised to discover. The well-preserved remains of a ship discovered in Mainz in central Germany several years ago suggest the importance of shipping on the Rhine as well as the often very simple construction of the vessels used.

Land transport was extremely expensive by comparison: The 225-pound (or so) capacity of a single- or double-axle oxcart with solid disk wheels

137 In the harbor of Ostia, grain was transferred from ocean-going vessels to smaller ships. Wall painting from Ostia. Rome, Vatican Museum.

(*plaustrum*) was relatively small and the average speed of 6 miles per day similarly slow. While the Roman empire was very well connected with technically superior roads, the roads served mostly to convey troops and to facilitate swift communica-

tion of reports and orders—almost the entire empire was dotted with relay stations at approximately 12-mile intervals for transport of letters and exchange of horses.

Thus, inside the empire, many smaller economic zones emerged, defined by the exchange of local goods. Within these zones, the markets of the larger cities became the emporium (loading point) for all sorts of goods. Direct long-distance trade or exchange of goods, beyond the given economic zone, was restricted to luxury goods or to specialized wares that were only produced in a few places and whose weight and size allowed relatively easy transportation. Among such goods in the 1st and 2nd centuries AD were the *Terra Sigillata* (107), a pottery made of a special clay. The pieces were produced in a number of sites in southern Gaul and from there carried throughout the empire. Likewise, *garum*, a spicy sauce made from fermented fish that was poured on almost every dish and whose preparation produced notoriously noxious odors in Pompeii and other cities, was also transported throughout the empire. The Monte Testaccio, a huge waste heap of amphora shards on the shore of the Tiber in Rome, is a still largely unread document of old Roman trade. The fragments reveal the place of origin and type of goods that were imported into Rome over hundreds of years.

138 Double-axle wagons were mostly drawn by a team of oxen, rather than horses, and were a slow means of transportation with a small load capacity. Relief from the Maria Hall in Carinthia, Austria.

27 BC – 284 AD

139 The 115-foot-high shard heap (Monte Testaccio) on the shores of the Tiber in Rome is a yet unexamined document of the ancient Roman economy. From the Republican period to the late ancient period, broken amphora, often bearing information about their origin and original contents, were deposited here.

140
Bronze sighting instrument (*groma*) of a Roman surveyor for determining two right-angled field axes. From Pompeii; Naples, National Museum.

141 Roman division of land areas into squares of 20 *actus* (approx. 2,260 x 2,263 feet), still visible today in Istria. Aerial photograph.

Surveying: Engineering as domination

Roman technology allowed the Romans to accomplish far more than the symbolic subjection of nature evident in their architecture (see p. 59); it also allowed and directly expressed their domination over land and people. An example of such politicized technology was land surveying, which proceeded from Rome as the center and, in the course of time, covered all acquired regions and integrated them into the Roman land register. The land in the empire was divided into regular squares or rectangles, whose boundaries in turn were marked by paths, ditches, or embankments. Especially during the decades between Caesar and Trajan, when the empire was growing apace, the conquered populations watched as armies of surveyors fitted with a *groma*—or measuring device—and a surveyor's staff heralded the arrival of the new culture of pragmatic Roman rationality.

The precision of Roman surveying and the rigor with which it took the conditions of the terrain in stride can be seen in the *limes* between Walldürn and Welzheim in Germany. This section runs over 50 miles across mountains and valleys in an absolutely straight line. Just how thoroughly the survey grid was etched into the landscape throughout the realm has been demonstrated by aerial photographs, for this ancient *centuriatio*—the measuring off and marking of the lands in blocks of 100 parcels of 50 hectares ranged along coordinate axes—is still used today as field boundaries.

Behind this painstakingly exact land surveying was the desire to incorporate newly conquered land as quickly as possible into the economic system, and thus into the tax base and administrative system. Since the growing armies were drawn from the landless classes, and these soldiers had to be paid upon leaving military service, it became necessary and expedient to distribute state land to veterans. To avoid the problems that had developed in the 1st century BC under Marius and Sulla, who were sharply criticized by the aristocracy for claiming the land of the dispossessed within Italy for soldiers' payment, newly won lands were immediately exploited as army payment. The dramatic dimensions of the problem can be seen clearly in the 7,600 square miles of land required to compensate the 34 legions of Augustus, who had defeated Caesar's assassins in the battle of Philippi in 42 BC.

Surveyed land was registered in cadastral books and could then be divided exactly, and just as exactly taxed. The remains of such a land register have been found in Orange, in southern France. Administrative and financial considerations, however, were by no means the only motives for Roman surveying. For the defeated peoples, the humiliating, almost physically tangible takeover and allocation of the land by means of the victors' new technology, which allowed them to overcome any obstacle, made the change of ownership abundantly clear. The art of the survey engineer became an instrument of domination.

142 Reconstruction of the Roman land demarcations in Provence, between Avignon and Orange, France.

27 BC – 284 AD

143 Roman surveyors at work: In teams of two or three men, territory incorporated into the empire was scrupulously measured and included into the Roman cadaster. Scene from "Asterix and the Satellite Town."

Water Conduits, Streets, and Bridges

144 Still in use today: Roman lighthouse of La Coruña on the northwest coast of Spain.

Nothing perhaps is more remarkable than the Roman infrastructure. In addition to settlements and cities, Rome's water pipes, streets, and bridges can be seen not only as manifestations of military conquest and the Roman domination of nature (see p. 59ff.), but as huge technical monuments, many of which are still existent today. Evidence of the Roman Imperium is particularly clear in the provinces. The original courses of many Roman roads are still in use today, though rarely in their original condition; many a thoroughfare in England, Scotland, and Wales, in Germany and in France, was originally a Roman road. Many authentic ancient bridges and even aqueducts are still in use. Certainly, their construction and maintenance over centuries is a striking technical achievement, but perhaps more impressive, if less well appreciated, are the complicated legal and administrative procedures that produced and sustained them. Transregional roads and water conduits had to be run across public land; to do so, the state needed first to acquire the land, sometimes through the right of eminent domain, which remains a fundamental law in many nations' legal systems. Often, long distance roads and aqueducts were built on the initiative, and sometimes as the donation, of wealthy magistrates or their families. Names like the Via Appia, Via Aemilia, Via Flavia, as well as the urban Roman water conduits such as Aqua Marcia, Aqua Julia, and Aqua Augusta testify to the various families' personal involvement.

Subsequent maintenance of public works was the responsibility of officials who either elicited fees from users according to various laws or drew the necessary funds from special community coffers. Within cities and towns, the roads branched out into private ways and the water flowed through underground pipes to fountains and taps that stood on almost every street

145 Still in use today: Roman bridge across the Tagus near Alcantara in western Spain. The keystone arches with their perfect distribution of weight allowed the Romans to build bridges with relatively large spans.

Water Conduits, Streets, and Bridges

corner; these marked the interface between public and private responsibility. It was illegal but quite common for people to tap into the 50- or 60-mile-long aqueducts for agricultural irrigation. Tapping, along with any number of breaks and leaks, was one reason for the often lamented water shortages. The Roman official Frontinus, responsible for the maintenance of the water conduits in Rome under Trajan, described in his book *de aquis urbis Roma* a plethora of legal and administrative details: "The Aqua Claudia is beset with special impairments. It delivers no more than 114,200 m³ of water to Rome, although its source provides 184,280 m³, a loss of 70,080 m³ per day." The threatened penalties were drastic: "Every person who breaks into canals, water channels, arched passages, lead and clay pipes, reservoirs and fountains shall be punished with 100 lashes" (Law of the Consul Crispinus, 9 BC, according to Frontinus).

147 A sectional drawing of the foundation of a Roman road.

For building large bridges and watercourses, poured cement technology (see p. 96ff.) was a necessary but not sufficient prerequisite; construction also required elaborate computation and leveling procedures to create the proper gradient, sometimes as slight as 3 feet in 3 miles. Equally important was the sovereign command of the principle of pressure lines which could overcome even 325-foot ascents. To bridge mountain chasms required both considerable skill from the workers and competent engineering to avoid collapse. River bridges built on swampy ground required ingenious foundations and experience in weight dispersion where precise dead reckoning was impossible. Roman road-building techniques truly approached modern standards. Roadways were normally 23 to 120 feet wide; they were dug out of the ground, the foundation was laid with stamped, sometimes mortared, layers of stone, and they were finally covered with fine pebbles, or even plastered. The road's profile had a slight camber, or arch, to it, so that water could run off into two side-ditches created by excavation.

146 Still in use today: Roman aqueduct of Tarragona in Spain bridges over a 650-foot-wide valley. The system was renovated in the 18th century.

202 AD Edict of Septimius Severus makes it legal to be a Christian, but illegal to become one

203 Arch of Septimius Severus on the Forum Romanum

212–216 Caracalla baths built in Rome

242 In Persia, Mani proclaims his religion (Manichaeism)

247 1,000th anniversary celebration of Rome

257–258 Persecution of the Christians

260 Edict of Gallienus; Christianity becomes a legal religion

271 Defensive wall around Rome (Aurelian Wall)

297 Edict against the Manichaeans

301 Currency (coin) reform and price ceiling set by Diocletian

305 Diocletian resigns and withdraws to retirement palace in Split

315 Beginning of the Arian heresy (theological dispute between Athanasius and Arius)

374–397 Ambrosius becomes bishop of Milan

ca. 375–380 Church of the Resurrection built in Jerusalem

386, 391–392 Edict allowing the plundering of heathen temples

393 Last Olympic games of the ancient world

453 Death of Attila

500 Theoderich occupies Rome

622 Beginning of the Islamic calendar; Muhammad relocated in Medina

800 Crowning of Charlemagne in Aix-la-Chapelle

284 – 565 AD

The crisis of the Roman empire in the 3rd century AD

Ever since the 18th century, modern historians have tended to look askance at the 3rd century AD: Up until the reign of Septimius Severus, the Roman empire is seen as prosperous and stable in all political, social, and economic areas. And then began an unstoppable decline. Certainly, there is archaeological evidence and there are historical records pointing to an epoch of collapse that was even recognized as such by its contemporaries. Political, military, and economic problems were entangled in an impenetrable morass to the point where even today it is unclear which phenomena should be seen as causes and which as effects.

A fundamental problem was the disintegration of the empire's borders. The north and the west in particular felt the force of the first great westward tribal migrations. Overpopulation and crop failures in northern and eastern Europe forced the emigration of entire tribes. This in turn led to an avalanche of relocations attended, as is so often the case, by bloodshed and war. The Herules, for example, who had been driven from Scandinavia in the 260s AD, pushed their way into the empire, leaving a trail of destruction through Greece. In spite of ever tightening border security (see p. 90ff), an immovable bulwark proved elusive. Humiliating defeats increased, in spite of tremendous military efforts, and large areas of the empire were lost. The first Roman emperor to fall was Decius in the battle near Abritus in 251; in 260 Valerian was captured by the Persians and died shortly thereafter, and between 270 and 275 Aurelianus had the city of Rome, still far removed from the scenes of battle,

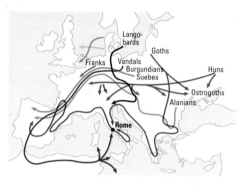

148 The great migrations of the 3rd–5th centuries AD: Important movements of individual tribes and ethnic groups.

encircled by an enormous defensive wall— a psychologically traumatic event for the city's inhabitants,

Closely related to these military problems was a breakdown in political structures. Again and again, generals were promoted by their legions to the position of regent; this meant that they not only had to struggle against enemy armies but also against many imperial "pretenders." The Senate, responsible for formally recognizing (and thus legitimating) each emperor, soon lost both perspective and influence over the 22 pretenders to the throne who appeared in sequence, in pairs, or in opposition to each other between 235 (the end of the Severine dynasty) and 284. To complete this picture of anarchy, individual usurpers proclaimed independent kingdoms within the Roman state.

That these events must have consequences for the administration as well as for the empire's social and economic conditions is clear. The ever-growing military machine swallowed immense sums of money, while the economic system came to a standstill. Cheap substitute money was coined by the ton to pay soldiers, and galloping inflation finished the job of destroying the money economy. The state and the administration passed and attempted to

284 - 565 AD

149 Emperor Galerius conquering the Persians, who beg for mercy as they surrender. Relief on a gold medallion. Berlin, State Museum, Coin Cabinet.

150 Septimius Severus with his wife and two sons. Family portraits, like this panel painting found in Egypt, represented the emperor's attempts to propagandize a new dynasty. His younger son, Geta, was deleted from the picture after he was assassinated as a rival by his older brother Caracalla and his memory fell victim to the *damnatio memoriae*.

151 The defensive wall started by the emperor Aurelianus in 271 AD was 12 miles long and almost 65 feet high in places. Even this bulwark was unable to protect Rome from occupation on several occasions in the 4th and 5th centuries.

284 – 565 AD

enforce new tax laws, but these laws had little effect beyond the resistance of the wealthy and the collapse of communal infrastructure (see pp. 113f).

These "phases of recession" in an empire founded on continuous expansion, however, were not necessarily perceived solely as a crisis. Even if hardly a single inhabitant of the empire was left untouched by the economic and social changes, these shifts in the established structures were oriented toward the future and opened up entirely new possibilities for many people. In 193 AD, Septimius Severus was named emperor. Severus came from north Africa and with his reign came a law extending equal rights of citizenship throughout the empire in 212. This undermined Italy's dominance of the empire and allowed more peripheral areas to develop into more important centers in their own right. Most of the "soldier emperors" of the 3rd century came from the provinces. The Senate in Rome lost its political influence and Roman nobility (by blood) no longer guaranteed high social position. Military rank or an individual clans' wealth became more accurate barometers of social prestige and carried more political weight than membership in one of the old Roman *gentes*. In fact, most complaints about the decaying condition of the empire

issued from these circles, who lost their preferred position during these years. For many of the less-well-off people, the collapse of certain qualities of the status quo opened up considerable new possibilities.

Searching for solutions: The empire as an object of reform

When the Illyrian general Diocletian was elevated to the throne by his Bithynia troops on November 17, 283 AD, a twenty-year period of reform was launched that led to a fundamental restoration and stabilization of the empire and that marked a new era of imperial rule.

The most pressing task for the new dynasty was to establish permanent security for the territory of the empire and to stabilize its power structures. Toward these ends, Diocletian developed a new form of government that installed at first two, and then later four, emperors with precisely defined competencies and areas of authority, with a clearly spelled out hierarchical structure. As "augustus," Diocletian enjoyed a rank equal with that of the god Jupiter; Maximian was also "augustus," but his restricted responsibilities placed him in the divine hierarchy at the secondary level of the god Hercules. Galerius and Constantius were each active as junior partner to an "augustus" and earned the rank of a "caesar." This tetrarchy was intended to provide for a regular transition in power, as the "augusti" stepped down and the *caesares* advanced to replace them. Despite its goal of providing stability and continuity of rule, Diocletian's innovation barely survived his own reign; it did, however, produce military success on all threatened borders and reestablish a homogenous empire. Under the tetrarchy, and beyond its short life, the empire was divided into four zones of governance, with three additional capitals declared in Milan,

152 The Aula Palace in Trier was built under Constantine in the early 4th century, when Trier was the northwestern part of the empire. The building was part of a cluster of palaces and served as the official site of court ceremonies.

The Roman Army

153 The Roman army attacking a walled city. Detail from an anonymous 17th-century French copper engraving.

The structure and organization of the Roman army underwent considerable changes from the early republic to the Late Antiquity. From the very beginning, the republican order of state was intimately aligned with the constitution of the army (see p. 30ff), which was fundamentally based on the military duty of all non-slaves, who were ranked by social position and wealth. Troops were organized according to need and demobilized as soon as a military action ended. Payment normally consisted of farmland grants in some newly founded *colonia*. The idea of maintaining a militia composed of all men subject to service remained *de jure* until into the Late Antiquity, but in fact it broke down in the 1st century BC with the creation of a professional army whose allegiance was far stronger toward their commander than toward the state of Rome. The extensive territorial enlargements of the 1st century AD required a standing army stationed in the provinces; the corps of soldiers consisted of both voluntary recruits and draftees. Finally, the crisis of the third century precipitated other changes: A complex military logistic with stationary and mobile troops, as well as reserves, evolved.

In the early period, the term "legion" designated all troops who fought in battle rows; later it meant a readily available force of 5,000 to 6,000 men subdivided into smaller groups (originally in maniples, later in ten cohorts composed of six centuries with 80 or 100 soldiers each). Often, the commander of the legion was not a soldier but an official—under the Republic, he was one of the consuls. The second in command would be

154 The Roman army taking revenge: Execution of the vanquished after the battle. Scene from the spiral relief of the Column of Marcus in Rome (180 AD) depicting the defensive battles of Marcus Aurelius against the invading Marcomanni.

The Roman Army

155 End of a brief military career: As illustrated on his tombstone, the legionnaire Genialis was the standard bearer carrying the picture of the emperor in the 7th Raetian cohort. He died at the age of 35.

an experienced practitioner, a legionary prefect who assisted with administration, organization, and military trail blazing and engineering. The prefect often took command in battles but did not bear the responsibility for the legion. Each legion had its own name, which was used not only in official documents but also as a brand for construction materials for forts; we have this penchant for organization and labeling to thank for our detailed overview of the stationing and movements of individual troops.

We tend today to have an exaggerated impression of the total size of the Roman army. In the 1st and 2nd centuries AD, there were a total of twenty-eight legions—that is, hardly 170,000 men. With the exception of crises, no more than two legions were allowed to be stationed in a single province; the conquest of Britain in 43 AD involved only four legions. In times of military necessity, however, the number of legions could be increased very quickly—under Diocletian there were more than sixty. An oversized standing military apparatus also served as a proven social-political method of providing wages for those without work or means; at the same time, however, a surplus military posed a danger, for a dissatisfied military could be a "state within a state," ready for a coup d'etat.

Attached to the infantry legions were auxiliary troops. These were special units of, for example, cavalry or archers. Originally, such specialized units were organized separately from among the allies of Rome and later incorporated into the military structure, while the soldiers were usually recruited from the provinces. The auxiliary troops had a nominal size of 500 men, but the total number varied; on the whole, their numbers probably equaled the total strength of the legions.

156 The Roman soldiers' tools were usually produced in their own workshops. Reconstructed military tools in the Saalburg.

157 Gold coins such as these with a value of 5 aurei (500 sesterce) with a portrait of Constantius enabled Romans to reestablish faith in the currency, even among the well-to-do. The currency reform raised the gold content of the aureus from 1/70 to 1/60 of a Roman pound, i.e., 1/10 of an ounce.

158 Symbol of governmental reform: The Tetrarchy under Diocletian is depicted as the visibly harmonious unity of four emperors. Venice, St. Mark's Cathedral.

Trier, and Thessalonica; this decentralization generally tended to undercut the hegemony of Rome itself and of Italy in general. Diocletian himself spent only a few weeks in Rome in the course of his twenty-year reign, and Italy lost its exemption from taxes and was divided into provinces. The climax of the process was the act of state in which the emperor Constantine removed the capital to Byzantium, known as *Nea Roma*, on May 11, 330. In general, decentralization proved a useful way of accommodating the centrifugal forces of diverse and conflicting religious beliefs and ethnic traditions within a single empire that had, in its expansion, become a multinational state, no longer strictly "Roman."

The reign of the tetrarchy was marked by many internal reforms geared toward resolution and restoration in all problematic areas, whether political, administrative, economic, military, or social. One element in the effort to strengthen the border security system was reform of the army. The provincial and district reforms (see p. 88ff) were accompanied by an administrative overhaul that guaranteed almost complete administration of the empire by means of a seemingly modern bureaucracy and implementation of tax reform by means of new penal laws, systems of control, and a collective liability. Taxes on real estate were eliminated, as were duties on farm animals and people. The inflationary monetary system was returned to a calculable basis through currency reform whereby the valuation of metal coins was increased in relation to the noble metals; this was an apparently necessary step, but it raised the value of all noble metals in circulation and thus resulted in a nominal increase in buying power. In order to curtail any uncontrolled jumps in prices, price ceilings were set by an edict in effect throughout the empire. Surviving inscriptions and papyri reveal over 1,400 prices for goods and services from which we have learned immeasureable details about economic transactions and relations.

Part and parcel of this era of reform were changes in court ceremony. Minutely specified rules dictated clothing regulations and social norms. The emperor from this point on bore the title *dominus et deus* ("lord and god"). The official public pomp and display became especially formalized. The schematic and stiff visual art of the period bears witness to this solidification of ceremonial norms. The principality once led by the *princeps* (a term adopted very deliberated by Augustus) was now a feudalistic domain under the *dominus et deus* whose political and administrative court officials were increasingly dissociated from the reality of the lives of the populace.

The Late Antiquity: Modern expression or historical epoch?

Modern accounts of the Late Antiquity that end with either the division of the Roman empire (395 AD), the collapse of the western half of the empire (476), or the death of Justinian (565) are following a convention of modern history. The time between Diocletian and Justinian (**161**) is considered as if it were a definable epoch that is then deemed either the decline of the earlier age that had kept itself in "bloom," or the "seed" of the Romanesque-Germanic and Byzantine Middle Ages. This interpretation can be traced back to the English historian Edward Gibbon's *History of the Decline and Fall of the Roman Empire*, which he wrote in six volumes between

159 Late ancient court ceremony: The silver plate from Madrid (Academy) shows Theodosius I (center) seated with his two princes (right and left) at the 10th anniversary of his reign in 388 AD. The hierarchy of the figures is demonstrated by the difference in size among the figures. The "portrait" of Theodosius is presented in a formally abstract style inside an aureole.

160 Late ancient court ceremony: The consul Aerobindus at the organizing of the Circus games in 506. These kinds of ivory tablets were produced as souvenirs. Zurich, State Museum.

284 – 565 AD

161 Late ancient court ceremony: Emperor Justinian and his attendants. Mosaic from the chancel of San Vitale in Ravenna. Mid-6th century AD.

1776 and 1788. When, in 1923, the German historian and philosopher Oswald Spengler wrote *The Decline of the West*, he positioned the Late Antiquity in the center of a cultural history of the first millennium; in so doing, Spengler revised the image of the period and offered an alternative evaluation, in an approach that uses artificial caesuras to divide history into discrete epochs.

It is doubtful, however, that those who lived in the Roman empire during these centuries would have thought of themselves as living in a Late Antique Roman period, or that the immediate present was an "interval" any more than we may define our own era in terms that are valid beyond a single decade or two. But the Late Antique Romans might be just as unlikely to consider themselves living in a "golden age." Even if there were those who thought of their times as decadent and of their society as on the verge of collapse, nonetheless, the Late Antiquity was generally not the "end of the ancient world," nor was it a "transition" to the Middle Ages. Like any other age, it was no more than a stage in a fluid process of gradual transition—a process that can be defined in terms of its results and described and understood quite without the aid of artificial epoch limits. The period-model of history has held a certain convenient charm for the historian, but it is, after all, only an artificial device. Certainly, the tendencies among historians and scholars to draw convenient lines of demarcation are just as problematic in the study of any era, but the conception of the "Late Antiquity" is especially questionable because it suggests a finite end to the ancient world that in fact never occurred.

Munera and urban flight: The late antique domain as image of the world

The Roman and imperial culture of the first two centuries AD was predominantly urban in character, but in the 3rd century the affluent families began to retreat from the cities and to develop their own domiciles and agricultural estates into magnificent noble residences. It doesn't really matter whether this development was a cause or a result of the crisis of these decades; the fact is that flight from the cities by the rich was most likely prompted by the burdensome fiscal policy of the state and that this policy had to become increasingly restrictive as the exodus from the cities of the wealthier class grew. Since the territorial expansion of the Roman empire had come to a halt and no new resources were available to exploit, the military could not be maintained with traditional state income.

A concrete reason for a withdrawal from the cities was the *munera*. Once a voluntary public office of the order of the decurions (see p. 76), it had long since become an obligation from which one could not escape as long as one lived in the city, and it could easily lead to financial ruin. The texts of various laws list in minute detail the public duties that had to be assumed and financed: funding for all administrative offices; mounting gladiator and theatrical shows; providing grain to the poor; maintaining water lines, streets, bridges, and city walls; operating the thermal baths; supporting one's wards and other de-

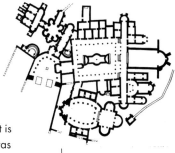

162 Villa of Piazza Armerina, built in the most isolated area of Sicily ca. 300 AD, was fitted with every possible comfort and luxury. Reconstructed layout.

163 Floor mosaic of the Villa of Piazza Armerina: Exotic animals are captured during an African expedition either for domestic decoration or for Circus games. Ca. 300 AD.

284 – 565 AD

164
Silver
serving platter
from a sumptuous table service; found near Augst (in the
vicinity of Basel, Switzerland).
The middle of the plate is
decorated with a picture of
an estate; in front are the
natural products of the estate.
Partially gilded relief, 4th
century AD. Augst, Roman
Museum.

165 Mosaic from the Villa of
Dominus Julius illustrating in
almost programmatic clarity
the estate, surrounded by
agricultural activities, as the
center of the world. 4th century AD. Tunis, Bardo Museum.

284 – 565 AD

pendents; and continually balancing the
public debt. The succession of the
munera was also precisely regulated.
According to the jurist Ulpianus, at
the beginning of the 3rd century,
"The governor had to be careful
that the services and honorary
offices ... were apportioned
equally according to age and rank
in the cities." The *Codex Theodosianus* from the 4th century is more
blunt: "Sons ... must assume the offices
of their fathers."

Flight from the city was the one legal way
for the wealthier circles to avoid this enforced
duty. But, because the coffers available to
cover the cities' public needs were steadily
shrinking, ultimately endangering the entire
infrastructure, such flight was legally banned:
"When the members of any *collegium* move to
another area," says the *Codex Theodosianus*,
"they must be compelled to return to carry out
their duties." Thus, attempts were made by
decree, even going so far as to forbid a
change of profession, to force an entire
society not only to conserve the status quo,
but to restore a status quo already passé into
the unforeseeable future. The effort represented
an unrealistic dogma that
spawned widespread
attempts at evasion.

Far from the cities, on country
estates with luxurious villas and
rich farms, life was easy and
undisturbed. The homes were
palatial, such as the villa near
Piazza Armerina in Sicily (**162,
163**), and fitted with every
comfort: Mosaics, wall paintings, heating, expensive

household fittings, a variety of baths and toilets, a kitchen and service wings, private chambers and visiting rooms formed the heart of the villa, which included far-ranging gardens. The farming industry that supported the estate, with its noise, mess, and stench, usually lay at a distance.

Against this background, withdrawal to the estates in the late third century developed into a regular lifestyle that was depicted in many paintings, mosaics, and silver utensils from the period. Such pictures illustrate a wide variety of economic activities and prestigious social ceremonies and yield a comprehensive image of life on the estates.

166 Proiecta's Silver toiletry box with two partially gilded reliefs. The artful pictures on the box and lid illustrate a festive marriage ceremony with Proiecta at the center. The ornamentation of the piece refers to its function in the life of the late antique upper class. 4th century AD. London, British Museum.

Rome and the Christians

From a modern point of view, probably no issue involving ancient Rome is more riddled with clichés than the relation of the Christian religion with the pre- or non-Christian state. Moreover, there is probably no issue around which attempts at a rational objectification become so dangerously embroiled with contemporary norms. The boundless sea of ancient Christian literature since the 3rd century is replete with stories of the repressive state machinery that persecuted the charitable, peace-loving, self-sacrificing Christians, that executed them or martyred them in other ways. The heathen literature itself reports vicious, direct persecutions of the Christians, especially in the 3rd century, but even in the days of Nero or Domitian. What actually was the central problem in the relationship between the Christians and the ancient Roman state—a relationship in which it seems today that the roles of victim and oppressor were undeniably shared?

284 – 565 AD

167 Christ as a worldly lord in magnificent robes. Pictures such as this revealed Christianity's religious and worldly claim to absolute rule. Apse mosaic from the Church of Saints Cosmos and Damian that had been remade from an originally pagan library. Ca. 530 AD.

From the establishment of the first sects in the hinterland of the Levantine coast around the 1st century BC, early Christendom was at first only one of many currents enriching the spectrum of Roman religion as the expansion of the empire brought it into contact with southern and eastern cultures (see p. 20ff). Despite their differences, however, it seems that the polytheistic religions managed to coexist with little difficulty; they even fused elements—gods, goddesses, myths, legends, rituals. But the introduction of monotheistic, hermetically closed religions that rigorously rejected the beliefs of others was far more problematic.

168 Baptismal room of a "house church" in Dura Europos on the Euphrates. Reconstruction, ca. 250 AD. New Haven, CT, Yale Gallery.

It wasn't just their defensive negation of all other religions and their assertion and dissemination of their own that brought the Roman state to feel resentful towards the Christians. The new Christian religion also had certain escapist tendencies that cut against the Roman grain. The idea of an earthly vale of tears and a heavenly paradise after death could weaken the relation of believers to the tangible present—to this life, this society, and this state. If believers in the new religion turned away from social duties with their political, social, and economic hierarchies and mechanisms, all rulers of all ages would be threatened and likely to launch countermeasures. This was precisely what happened when, in ancient Greece, the state moved to suppress the similarly structured Orphic-Pythagorean religious cults, or when the Romans also persecuted the monotheistic Manichaeans in the Late Antiquity.

From Palestine and Egypt, Christianity spread over Asia Minor and Greece into the western parts of the empire. Such dissemination in the 1st and 2nd centuries AD was possible only because the empire's internal stability was recognized so absolutely. In the 3rd century, Christianity gained momentum, becoming a mass phenomenon, but it was only after the emperor Constantine actually decreed it the official state religion at the Council of Nicea in 325 AD that a hierarchically structured and state-governed organization formed. Now the religion was unified and codified—processes that led to dogmas but also to a proliferation of schisms and sects. An ecclesiastical hierarchy headed by a pope evolved along with a regulated liturgy and various suborganizations—synods, councils, parishes, even national churches. Christianity's ongoing success started here and was unstoppable, even against occasional attempts to revert to heathendom, as happened under Julian (361–363 AD) who was later branded "the Apostate."

The new Christian state reacted to religious and social conflicts with far more rigor than the pre-Christian state had exercised toward Christianity in its early days. The dogma of the "sole truth" prompted fanatical persecutions, first of individual Judeo-Christian splinter groups, but also, especially under Theodosius (379–395) and Justinian (527–565), to organized and state-sanctioned massacres of heathens—the first signs of a fundamental

169 Basilica of San Paolo fuori le muri in Rome is a typical martyr's church, erected on the site of the death of the apostle. Built under the emperor Theodosius in the late 4th century AD, the basilica was restored after the fire on July 16, 1823. 18th-century engraving by Piranesi.

170 Basilica B in Philippi in northeast Greece, 6th century AD. The basilicas and bishop's palace formed a single conglomerate with almost the size and contents of a city.

284 – 565 AD

The Catacombs

171 Grave plate marker made of gold glass with an illustration of Saint Agnes in the Panfilo catacombs in Rome. The picture was made by placing a gold leaf etching within a thin glass layer. 4th century AD.

Next to the extensive system of sewers under the city of Paris, the network of more than seventy catacombs covering almost 100 miles of corridors under the city of Rome is the most famous monument of underground excavation in a European metropolis. This much is fairly common knowledge. What is less known is that only a part of these Christian and Jewish graveyards was originally underground and that the word catacomb was first used to describe them in the Middle Ages; it was borrowed from the remaining underground cemetery of San Sebastiano with the local nickname *ad catacumbas* ("in valley bottom") on the Via Appia. The first of these burial places were established on private grounds around 150 AD as family tombs for the wealthy or for

members of a burial society. Whether or not these earliest locations were reserved exclusively for Christians remains unclear.

The cemetery was later transferred to community ownership. Individual graves of saints or martyrs became loci for devotion or pilgrimages, and therefore sometimes the seed of later church buildings. The most famous of these is probably St. Peter's Cathedral, which was built over the extensive catacombs that are supposed to contain the grave of St. Peter.

After the 10th century, most of the catacombs were simply forgotten, not to be rediscovered again until around 1600. The Christian view of death—which was responsible for the exclusion of Christians from traditional burial places—remained suspect throughout the heathen classic world (see p. 116). There is a longstanding Christian tradition/legend that, in times of suppression, Christians withdrew in fear into their underground cemeteries to pray and hold their services, or even that they

172 Christ as teacher among the apostles. Fresco from the Domitilla catacomb, ca. 350 AD.

The Catacombs

hid there over longer stretches of time; this, however, is little more than a myth that demonizes the heathens. But the short-term restrictions placed on Christians in the latter half of the 3rd century AD became entrenched clichés in paintings, book illustrations, and movies such as *Quo Vadis?*

The catacombs were built by special grave diggers called *fossores*, following a defined plan; they were designed either as a broadly branching system stemming out of a main hall, or as a compact grid with two parallel halls connected by several passages. The passages, dug into the soft tuff stone, were stable, with top openings for air and light, as well as for entry, at regular spaces. The shortage of space was solved by digging deeper; the catacombs thus developed into multistory labyrinths.

Branching out from the passages were the individual burial sites. These were complete rooms with entrance façades and interior niches for more elaborate coffin burials. The rooms also functioned as family tombs and provided a place for burial rituals such as the funeral meal or the celebration of the Eucharist. Many passages were lined with several tiers of small recessed wall chambers, or *loculi*, for the bodies of the dead. Stone slabs, or sometimes tiles, were set

173 Passage in the Panfilo catacomb containing stacked niche graves. 4th century AD.

over the chambers to seal the tombs, just as one can see today in many Italian cemeteries.

The *loculi* were marked for identification and sometimes adorned with a piece of golden glass (**171**), a coin stuck into the mortar of the slab, or with graffiti. After the 3rd century AD, the tombs were more commonly decorated with wall paintings. Thus, the catacombs offer a broad spectrum of pictures whose themes were at first wholly in the tradition of ancient Roman heathen art. Only after Christianity became a state religion did such painting freeze into a schematic "official" Christian iconography. Approximately half of the urban Roman catacombs, and a similar proportion of those in other cities (such as Split, Arles, or Trier) contain paintings of sometimes considerable splendor and constitute an extremely important contribution to early Christian art and religious history.

174 Pictures of the ecclesiastical hierarchy are formally reminiscent of the late ancient ceremony (compare with **161**). Above, the bishop as teacher; next to him, the deacon (seated), and the priests (standing). Below, the lower orders of clergy with their typical attributes, also portrayed in hierarchical order. Miniature from the Ragnaldus Sacrament, 9th century AD. Autun, Bibliotèque Municipale.

Christian intolerance that would later become manifest in the crusades and the Inquisition. During the reign of Justinian, all heathen temples were closed and the old schools of philosophy were outlawed. Great numbers of shrines were taken, plundered and pillaged. The church of the empire now claimed all magnificence for itself and grew economically powerful during this time.

Early Christian churches, especially in Rome, Constantinople, and Thessalonica, still demonstrate the material wealth of the official church. Their spacious architecture, magnificent, gilded mosaic trim, and jewel-like decorations are both signs of wealth and symbols of glory and power. At the same time, the Christian architecture and art work manifest the transition from a more collective movement to an autocratic religious monopoly. "House churches," such as those from Dura Europos on the Euphrates (**168**), which existed everywhere until into the 3rd century, reveal the humble beginnings of individual communities that gathered privately for prayer and services. The large building conglomerates of the 4th and 5th centuries which, like those in Philippi or Nea Anchialos in Greece, could form regular church-cities, illuminate the growth of communities and economic potential with just as much force as do the pompous buildings of Rome, Ravenna, Thessalonica, or Constantinople.

The heirs of ancient Rome: Byzantium, Arab world, and Langobardic-western culture

Many historians subscribe to the view that, after the Roman empire was divided into an eastern and a western half in 395, and after attempts at reunification with the death of Justinian in 565 failed, the empire broke permanently apart into a Germanic-Latin west and a Byzantine east, and that both regions constituted the legitimate heirs of ancient Rome. This view, however, with its convenient foundation dates based on historical caesuras that are thoroughly consistent with an epoch-oriented modern approach to history (see p. 111ff), is arguably wrong. If one steps away from the details of the history of events and looks at the total geographical area of the Roman empire circa 800 AD, it is clear that there were not two, but three, cultural offshoots, each of which in its own way perpetuated the established structures of Rome and transformed them according to their own need. The third heir of Rome, sibling (as it were) of the Latin-western and Byzantine-eastern cultural spheres, was the Islamic world in the southeast of the former expansive empire.

Islam was born, at first with little fanfare or notice, in the seventh century on the Arabian peninsula. It soon spread to the near East and then along the north African Mediterranean coast and to Spain. In the process, it absorbed various Christian-Jewish currents but also underwent several divisions. This course of events has often been pejoratively interpreted as a long string of militaristic conquests conducted by a sickly foreign culture, and compared with phenomena like the "Hunnish storm"—a polemical Christian point of view that also accounts for the

175 The more than 143-foot half-round dome of the Pantheon in Rome was built under Hadrian. In both its architectural technology and its equation of the heavenly dome with the realm of the gods, the Pantheon became a model that was borrowed in various forms by all of the cultures that succeeded Rome. Painting by G. P. Pannini, ca. 1740. Washington, DC, National Gallery of Art.

176 Byzantium from the Islamic point of view: View of Constantinople, illustration from Nashu ash-Shilahe al-Matrake, *Description of the Campaigns of Sultan Suleiman*, 1537. Istanbul, University Library.

284 – 565 AD

177 Dome of the Hagia Sophia in Constantinople. Completed in 537 AD, the dome collapsed in 558 and was rebuilt in steep profile to ornament the city's most famous palace church, which was also the center of Eastern Orthodox Christianity. The building has been a Moslem mosque since 1453.

western world's general failure to give the Arabic-Islamic share of the classic inheritance its due. A good deal of the surviving knowledge of medicine, engineering, and astronomy and of the many ancient texts in these fields have been passed down only by way of the Arabic world.

The Byzantine empire has been accurately and concisely described by historian Georg Ostrogorsky: "Roman state, Greek culture, and Christian faith are the main sources of Byzantine development. If one of these elements is taken away, the Byzantine system becomes impossible. This synthesis was made possible by the removal of the weight of the empire toward the east. ... Byzantine history is merely a new era of Roman history, and the Byzantine state only a con-tinuation of the old Imperium Romanum. ... The Byzantines always called themselves Romans, their emperors considered themselves Roman rulers, Roman traditions of state ruled until the end their political thinking and dealing" (*Byzantine History*, Munich: 1952, p. 22). Until the late Middle Ages, a smaller version of Rome survived inside the Byzantine empire. Not until 1461, with the Turks' overthrow of the imperial realm of Trebizond were the last traces

178 View into the dome of the Church Panhagia Pari-goritissa in Arta (northwest Greece). This famous Byzantine church consists in part of building elements of an abandoned Roman city in the vicinity. An image of Christ ornaments the dome. 13th century.

284 – 565 AD

of Roman culture absorbed into the Ottoman state. In almost all areas of life—in culture, religion, politics, the economy, justice, and administration—ancient Roman structures, albeit in changing forms, remained alive, and the greatest portion of knowledge surviving from Roman antiquity comes from this sphere of Byzantine culture.

While the Byzantine empire and the Islamic-Arabic world proved to be relatively homogenous structures in spite of all their conflicts and challenges, it took several hundred years for the Latin-western hemisphere to coalesce into a cultural unity after the fall of the western Roman empire and the great migrations of the 4th and 5th centuries—even if the Catholic church claims an unbroken papal continuity from Peter to the present day. Goths (early Germanic tribes in southern France up to the Loire), Franks (Germanic tribes along the Rhine), and Langobards (Lombards, in the area that is now Hungary and eastern Austria) all had their own cultural identities. Outside the Byzantine empire, western Christianity had to make many efforts, either by missionary activity or by violence, to reestablish its universal status as a force for social unity. Not until around 800, with the empire of Charlemagne, did a large, Latin-western identity emerge; its relation to classical Rome, however, was very complicated and certainly the most alienated of the three "heirs" because of the array of independent cultural identities and historical discontinuities in the West.

179 The Dome of St. Peter's in Rome is the center of Latin-western Christianity. Dating from the second half of the 16th century, the height of the dome is strongly exaggerated in comparison with the half-round form of the Pantheon.

180 The Dome of the Rock in Jerusalem is visible from afar. Built ca. 700.

284 – 565 AD

182 The folding stool of Roman officials (*sella curulis*) remained a symbol for the authority of the law in later ages. This well-preserved bronze exemplar dating from the 6th century AD served the Merovingian king Dagobert as a throne. Paris, Cabinet des Médailles.

Byzantine empire, where, however, other standards such as the Syrian-Roman law book (which was later used in the Islamic world) were never completely replaced. When the Byzantine state vanished, the Roman system of law was completely eradicated through the fundamentally different structure of Ottoman law.

In the western-Latin world, in addition to canonical church law, a simplified system of Roman law was used for the simple reason that these vestiges of Roman law enabled Gothic or Burgundian kings most easily to regulate the conditions of those of their subjects who were still "Romanized." The basis of the "vulgar law" was in fact the subsumed Codex from the reign of Theodosius, which had been a target of Justinian reform. This Theodosian law was mixed with Gothic-Frankish-Langobardian elements. Between the time of the great migration and the late Middle Ages, most Roman law standards were forgotten, not to be rediscovered until a complete handwritten manuscript of the Justinian *corpus juris* was found. The first laws schools in Pavia and Bologna, founded in the 11th century following this very discovery, translated and commented upon ancient law. Roman law, thus, became a scholarly subject that in turn influenced the development of the city-states of the Renaissance. It also served as

183 The Roman emperor Justinian had all valid Roman legal standards codified. This *corpus juris*, the basis of the Roman law tradition, is still in use today. Mosaic from the Church of San Vitale, Ravenna. Mid-6th century AD.

5th century – today

a basis for the Roman-imperial law adopted by monarchs such as the Staufers, and even for secular and liturgical aspects of the Catholic Church.

Roman law has been dynamically applied ever since its Renaissance revival under changing circumstances. Traditional rules, such as those concerned with slavery, were simply dismissed. Even countries that attempted to develop entirely new principles in the wake of the Enlightenment referred to Roman law as a pattern. The completely different system of common law prevalent in England and the United States is based on precedent and actually represents an exception within the Latin-western culture.

Ancient artifacts

The images of rulers, whether in sculpture, jewelry, or images stamped on coins, became collectors' items of considerable value, especially for a complete set of the Roman emperors; such was the fervor for the images that many a collector settled for modern imitations in "antique style" to fill gaps in his collection. While such imitations were probably not originally intended to be fraudulent, but merely to supply a desired commodity (just as the Romans themselves were quite content to own knock-offs of Greek art), their mixing into authentic ancient collections has led to a certain amount of difficulty for subsequent researchers.

Many portrait galleries as well as coin and precious stone collections have been set up in the courts of princes and kings since the Middle Ages. The church also, with its own monarchy-like hierarchy,

184 The Lothar Cross from the Aix-la-Chapelle Cathedral treasure. The golden processional cross containing an ancient cameo with the portrait of Augustus expressed the donor's desire to be seen as a legitimate successor to the Roman emperors.

5th century – today

127

185 Unknown ruler, 5th–7th century. This bronze statue, in the style of the sculpted portraits of the ancient Roman emperors, was discovered in the harbor of the Apulian city Barletta in 1309, restored, and placed in front of the cathedral. The cross held in the right hand is an addition, and impressively demonstrated how worldly gestures of domination could be adapted by the church.

showed a distinct taste for Roman art and artifacts. For example, the Cross of Lothar from the cathedral treasure chamber in Aix-la-Chapelle (**184**) is typical of a church collection: in the middle of this 10th-century insignia of church power is a rich cameo of Augustus.

Ancient memorials, souvenirs, and artifacts were thus recycled and adopted for topical purposes. But this was not the only manner of Roman endurance. Since the early Middle Ages, rulers attempted to "ennoble" their own image by means of classic pictorial formulas. Even in the noncourtly circles of the urban upper classes and local magistrates, it was fashionable to refer in art, style, and manner to the antique rulers. Where no descriptions or images of a ruler survived to guide new depictions, artists of course let loose their own fantastic imaginations. In the different series of pictures of Roman and post-classic emperors on the 15th- and 16th-century wooden beam ceilings in Lüneburg, Germany, individual emperors can be identified by inscriptions and brief biographic details (**186**); how like they are to their original sources is anybody's guess.

With the ancient world serving as a model for contemporary culture, it was not long before the antique monuments and images

186 The Roman emperor Otho. Fantasy image of a wooden beam ceiling containing a cycle of pictures of Roman and postancient rulers. From the house of a Lüneburg citizen, Grosse Bäckerstrasse 28, after 1534.

themselves became the direct objects of a kind of ideologically based exploitation. In short, the first antique collections, forerunners of modern museums, came into being. Rome and the provinces of the empire from then on were plundered regularly. Emperors and kings were not the only ones caught up in the collecting whirlwind; the popes in particular steadily added to their growing Vatican collections. The courts and the church in the 17th and 18th centuries especially amassed notable collections of ancient articles from which, it was hoped, their own glory and brilliance could be reflected. Even among the lower echelons of the aristocracy—the lesser princes, dukes, counts, viscounts—and even the country nobility such as the Count of Wallmoden-Gimborn from an illegitimate line of the Hanoverian Elector, all competed for treasures to impress the world with their wealth and taste. That such collections held considerable value and could become an issue of national prestige became clear during the Napoleonic wars. Antique art became first-class war booty (**187**). Napoleon's troops plundered the treasures of Egypt in a massive raid for spoils and went on to ravish the already centuries-old museum collections of Rome itself during the conquest of Italy in 1796–97. In a magnificent triumphal march, planned in every detail to replicate those described in ancient Roman reports, Napoleon's troops presented their war booty, including extremely famous works of ancient art like the "Laokoon" and the "Apollo Belvedere" from the Vatican, to the people of Paris in 1810, and then placed it all in a

187 Ancient art as modern war booty: Triumphal procession with captured antiques from all over Europe paraded through Paris in 1810. This segment shows Apollo Belvedere from the Vatican in Rome. Sketch for the frieze of an ornamented vase from the porcelain manufacture in Sèvres.

5th century – today

129

Roman Remains in the Vicissitudes of Time

188 Section from Giovanni Paolo Pannini's "Roma Antica," 1756/57. Stuttgart State Gallery. The painting shows an imaginary gallery with pictures of the ancient Roman buildings based on a variety of contemporary evidence. Such pictures from the 18th century reveal the prevailing value for Roman architecture.

The remains of Roman antiquity lay unburied in piles where they had fallen. Through the ages they were available for the practical needs of the people. Even when ancient goods were sometimes destroyed, it was rarely out of malevolence but more the byproduct of an unbiased use of the materials for people's present-day needs.

(How much have we discarded or destroyed from dubious legacies handed down in our families or our homes that might one day prove valuable?) It is our museum-generated vision that has turned such things into sacred "cultural objects." Yet at the same time, even the preservationist perspective of the museum culture has accepted

Roman Remains in the Vicissitudes of Time

the fact that supposedly archaeological, scientific activities have caused great and irreparable damage to the memorials and artifacts through restoration, through the "cleaning" of history. Ancient marble sculptures were burned to produce calcium, an important building material through the centuries, and bronze sculptures were so commonly melted down into weapons or other utensils that bronze finds are today rare exceptions. Such deeds, ironically, have posed fewer obstacles to our knowledge of the antique world than has the scattering and sequestering of ancient remains in the museums of the world. By gathering the objects into museums, curators and their agents have often erased the connections among the articles, yet the practice continues unquestioned in the name of science.

Roman architecture and infrastructure have continued to be used through the centuries. Roman cadastral records and field boundaries (see p. 100ff) have remained visible into the modern age and are sometimes used to delineate land ownership to this day. Roman water conduits, bridges, and streets still carry water, span rivers, and carry travelers across terrain, sometimes with hardly any modification over the centuries. Entire modern settlements lay like a cork on top of ancient structures. The Piazza Mercato, center of the Tuscan city of Lucca (190), still has the form of the original Roman amphitheater in the arrangement of the surrounding houses; the Piazza Navona in Rome, in spite of homogeneous Baroque decoration,

189 Temple of Antoninus Pius and Faustina, built in 141 AD, transformed into a church in the 12th century. The ancient front columns were exposed in 1536 and a baroque façade was added in 1602. Thus, an ancient temple and a modern church were merged into an architectural whole.

Roman Remains in the Vicissitudes of Time

190 The center of the Tuscan city Lucca derived from the structure of a Roman amphitheater.

still reveals the elongated Circus of Domitian that once stood there; and the semicircular forms of various Roman theaters remain visible through the apartment houses constructed in the Middle Ages. Even the Colosseum, today the largest of Rome's ruins, continued to be inhabited until the 18th century.

When antique buildings were converted into Christian churches, it may have seemed that they were being preserved in the process, but in fact it was, as usual, a convenient way simply to recycle the ancient architecture. Old walls were radically renovated to serve their new purposes. For example, the entrance to Greek temples was moved from its customary position on the east wall to the west side of the building, while an apse was built into the east and all traces of paganism were ferreted out and erased. Sometimes

Roman Remains in the Vicissitudes of Time

the fusion of ancient and modern architectural forms produced a cacophony of styles, as in the Temple of Antoninus Pius and Faustina in Rome (189). Indeed, the Pantheon itself, the most famous Roman temple, was remodeled into a Christian church in 608.

Finally, ancient structures were appropriated and redesigned for military use. Around 400 AD, Hadrian's mausoleum was incorporated into the city wall as an outpost. It was later renamed the Sant' Angelo and became the bulwark of the Vatican.

The furious plundering of antiquity was the order of the day. Ruins like the layout of the Roman city by Xanten, only a few hundred yards away from the medieval new city, were systematically quarried. All usable building material was either carted off to a new site or sold off. Ancient stones from Xanten have been found as far away as northern Germany where they were used in the cathedral at Schleswig. A conservationist way of thinking about architecture emerged relatively late, in the 18th century. Giovanni Paolo Pannini's painting *Roma Antica* of 1756–57 (188) depicts an entire gallery of paintings of ancient Roman ruins within an imaginary building. This, as well as Pannini's *Interior of the Pantheon*—a similar projection of historical reconstruction—is a document of the transformed attitude.

191   Several stories were added to the Marcellus theater, built in 12 BC in Rome, and the building was turned into a habitable palazzo.

192   Excavations of ancient Roman artifacts near Xanten, Germany, engraving from 1839. The goal of the work at this time was to search for treasure and for building materials that could be reused—not for scientific knowledge.

133

193 Ancient Rome was held fast by layers of later architectural sediment. Copper engraving of the Forum Romanum (honorary arch of Septimius Severus in the foreground) by Giovanni Battista Piranesi, ca. 1750.

specially redesigned gallery of the Louvre, called the Musée Napoleon. After protracted diplomatic negotiations, not untinged with hostility at times, the booty was eventually returned to its original custodians. Similar efforts are being made even today to return plundered art or sacred objects to their rightful owners, as European art seized by the Nazis is being turned up and returned to the museums of Europe, or as Native American objects are being removed from natural history museums and returned to surviving members of the various tribes.

Lasting beauty and elemental greatness: Ancient Rome and the cult of ruins

Giovanni Battista Piranesi (1720–78; **193**) was an Italian artist of the 18th century whose work was dominated by his topographical etchings and his love of classical antiquities. His famous etchings and engravings depicted Rome as a wildly romantic place filled with enchanted ruins and ancient remains that had "grown" deep into the earth. Rome lay in ruins, and the modern age, which had

194 *Capriccio with the Colosseum*, oil painting by Bernardo Bellotto, known as Canaletto, 1742–47. Rome is depicted as a mystical site, covered with ruins and vaguely folkloric people. Parma, National Gallery.

5th century – today

134

grown in overwhelming layers around it, becomes a physically discernible component of "burial," while at the same time exuding its own romantic atmosphere. The artist was trained as an architect and at one time worked for artists who made stage sets; his stage-set-like depictions of Rome were, on the one hand, influenced by the engravings of Marten van Heemskerck, Giovanni Antonio Dosio, Hieronymus Cock and Etienne du Pérac, and, on the other hand, inspired a spate of imitations in the late 18th and 19th centuries. Piranesi offered a portentous view of the ancient world: The ruins became a symbol simultaneously of transitoriness and permanence. The excavations that were already being conducted at the time were adjudged, as described in letters written by Wilhelm von Humboldt as envoy to the Vatican in the early 19th century, disturbing, as modernism pillaging the spirit of romance. On the other hand, the excavations of Herculaneum and Pompeii were themselves stirring a romantic fervor for things classical and ancient.

195 Ruin as model. The domed hall in the Roman Licinian Gardens, which were created in the 4th century AD, were copied by a German author of historical fiction as a ruin. An engraving by Piranesi served as the pattern for the model made of cork. Aschaffenburg, Palace.

This image of ruins became a metaphor for antiquity per se. Although a technically superior structure like the Colosseum (**194**) certainly suffered from the years, it nonetheless shook its fist "undefeated" in the face of time. The once great Roman buildings and monu-

5th century – today

> "If you thoroughly immerse yourself in the transitory and in ruins, though these ruins are the detritus of an [entire] world, then you will have an idea of the impression Rome makes on me. The first feeling is melancholy, but the immensity of what has been lost gives a grandeur to the melancholy, which then lightens. ... Rome is simultaneously the symbol of the transitoriness and the contininuity of the world."

> Wilhelm von Humboldt in a letter from Rome
> to Christian Gottfried Körner, June 8, 1805

135

ments, as well as the idealization of the "historicism" of antiquity in and of itself, became important as exemplifying the strength and glory of the structures precisely through their indestructibility (even when in ruins). Piranesi's hundreds of etchings of Rome and the prolific work of other Roman landscape artists document this "Romephilia." Models made out of cork or wood (**195**) showing

196 Ancient Rome as artificial ruins: The "Mountain of Ruins" in the park of Sanssouci palace, constructed in 1745 from a design by Georg von Knobelsdorff.

ancient buildings in their ruined state or, less often, in reconstructions of the buildings intact, helped spread this image of Rome throughout the world.

Ruin as a synonym for the ancient developed into such a powerfully effective topos that it became fashionable for kings and princes to construct artificial ruins at court as a feature in their parks or gardens (**196**). Pursuit of the ancient became a kind of bucolic courtly pastime, comparable to the toy world of Marie Antoinette in Versailles. "Modern" ruins served as the stage settings for garden parties and similar celebrations.

Rome as utopia: The American and the French Revolutions

Up until the middle of the 18th century, antiquity was perceived and accepted almost exclusively in terms of the period of the Roman empire. Indeed, the centuries of the empire were seen as a paradigmatic epoch with constituent ecclesiastical and imperial structures. This view changed somewhat around 1750 when this centuries-old perspective became subject to a more relativistic consideration and in the process opened up new ways of perceiving and interpreting the antique. Behind this change was the increasingly comprehensive critique of absolutist and feudal monarchies in the wake of the Enlightenment as well as the growing self-awareness of the middle classes.

Against the traditional ideal of imperial Rome, two alternative concepts emerged. It is no accident that it was precisely at this time, in this political and social climate, that ancient Greek culture was both "rediscovered" and liberated after lying shrouded for centuries within the Ottoman empire. With the eruption on the scene of Greek culture, art, and philosophy, the western understanding of the ancient world took a radical turn. The ancient world was no longer defined by the mere littany of emperors and their courtly arts, of techno-

197 Jacques-Louis David, *The Oath of the Horatii*, 1784, Paris, Louvre. A mythologized quarrel between families in early Rome becomes a revolutionary and patriotic gesture of armament in David's oil painting.

198 The Tempio Malatestiano in Rimini with a Roman façade finished by Leon Battista Alberti before 1468.

The image of the ancient world that persisted throughout the Middle Ages and has been handed down to the modern era has been largely pieced together from literary tradition. Texts by ancient authors were copied and recopied in monasteries, stored in libraries, and studied by members of the social elite. Collections of ancient laws, philosophical tracts, and theoretical treatises on the arts exerted tremendous influence on subsequent generations, and so shaped perceptions of the ancient world. With very few exceptions, the actual relics and artifacts—the sculpture, the buildings, the jewelry, the coins—were barely considered in the generation of these views.

Filippo Brunelleschi (1377–1446) of Florence, the first great Italian Renaissance architect, intensively studied the details of urban Roman architecture when planning the dome of the Florentine cathedral. He and Italian master builder Leone Battista Alberti (1404–72) were among the first to focus on the physical legacy of ancient Rome not only theoretically but in practical terms as well. Brunelleschi and Alberti together considered literary descriptions with scholastic attention, but they also looked at the surviving relics of the old city. When a copy of the *de architectura libri decem* by the ancient Roman architect Vitruvius was discovered in the monastery at St. Gallen in Switzerland, the text quickly became a

... Motifs in Renaissance Architecture and Drawing

reference for all Renaissance master builders. The ancient text was quickly translated, printed, and distributed. Inspired by Vitruvius, Alberti himself wrote *De re aedificatoria* (About Building), which he completed in 1452; his text, like that of Vitruvius, was divided into ten books and formulated in complex Latin. Alberti's interest in ancient construction principles went beyond his eager adoption of the ancient Roman's written precepts; Alberti studied the ruins themselves and used them as models for his own work. Although the Tempio Malatestiano in Rimini (**198**) was left unfinished in 1468 when its patron died, Alberti was able to fulfill his contract to provide the old Gothic church with a new façade. His design was patterned after the nearby antique arch for Augustus (**199**), which he copied exactly as a central motif for the church façade. This simple importation of an ancient motif suggests the appeal of Roman symbols of

fame in new, clerical applications. The patron of the work, the prince Sigismondo Pandolfo Malatesta, celebrated the façade in the manner of an ancient ruler.

Ancient buildings were frequently the subject matter of draftsmen in the late Renaissance; these artists were chiefly interested in structures that served an important function (such as city gates) or that bore significant symbolic weight (such as temple façades and memorial arches). The body of such drawings and other renderings from the 15th century bear witness to the Italian

199 The ancient honorary arch for Augustus in Rimini served as model for the front façade of Alberti's Tempio Malatestiano.

Renaissance efforts to grapple with their Roman inheritance. At the same time, they provide records of buildings and conditions that have since been irretrievably lost. It was at this same time that we can make out the germinating seeds of a trend to weave the surviving monuments into an idealization of the present based on the antique world. This development peaked in the reverent attitudes toward classic antiquity that dominated in the 18th and 19th centuries.

One century after Alberti, Andrea Palladio (1508–80) of Padua developed an architectural form that was considered a perfect synthesis of Renaissance and ancient structures. Palladio's views on antique architecture, which he comprehensively expounded in his *Four Books on Architecture* (published in 1570 in Italian and translated soon thereafter into eagerly awaited foreign-language editions), were partly derived from the theories of Vitruvius, but also, increasingly, from his own direct scrutiny of Roman ruins. His 1554 *The Roman Antiquities* remained unparalleled in its details for over a hundred years.

Like Alberti before him, Palladio also passed down many errors regarding the details of ancient forms. Where Alberti's relatively small-scale architectural analysis remained largely theoretical, Palladio designed and built many buildings,

200 Drawings like this 16th-century piece by Jean Gertraux of the Augustus arch in Arles, France, are of particular documentary value today. The ancient monument was torn down, with not a trace left behind, in the 17th century.

201 Andrea Palladio built many, many villas, such as this one designed for Giorgio Cornaro near Treviso, in northern Italy. The one- or two-story façades were fitted with columns as Palladio imagined would be authentic for ancient Rome.

including many villas in northern Italy. His striking synthesis was regarded as the sole and absolute form of antique imitation until the 18th century. Outside Italy, Palladio's architectural forms were copied and popularized with particular energy by English architects Inigo Jones (1573–1652) and the Earl of Burlington (1694–1753). Only after later, renewed study of ancient models did Palladianism and neo-Palladianism slowly decline toward the end of the 18th century.

logy and martial arts, for now the world heard about and saw the pictures and buildings of democratic city-states like Athens. Initially nurtured in England as a form of aristocratic escapism, this ideal traveled to the continent in the form of a partly revolutionary, partly bourgeois-romantic, but always utopian image of freedom and generosity. This longing for "noble simplicity and silent greatness," in Winckelmann's enthusiastic characterization of Greek art, soon blossomed into a virtual "Grecomania," which soon mutated in central Europe into a classicism respectful of authority.

There was an alternative to this Grecomania. Based upon the republican (pre-empire) ideals of ancient Rome, an antimonarchical concept for political activity grew. Its results would be felt especially in France and in the thirteen colonies of the English crown in America.

The French Enlightenment as well as the American independence movement drew upon 17th-century English political philosophy and, to a large degree, upon the Roman republican understanding of the state. Baron Charles de Montesquieu, significant as both a writer and a philosopher prior to the French Revolution, laid out the foundation for an alternative to the *ancien regime* of the absolute monarchs in his 1734 *Observations on the Greatness of Rome and the Reasons for its Downfall*. Montesquieu demanded a separation of state powers and called for an understanding of state and governmental responsibility that would encompass not only political considerations, but social, economic, legal, and moral concerns as well. Thus, a modern democratic

202 Ancient Rome as victory memorial: The Arc de Triomphe de Caroussel was built near the Louvre in Paris between 1806 and 1808 in celebration of the victories of Napoleon. It was copied from the ancient honorary arch for Septimius Severus in the Roman Forum.

vision took form for the first time with reference to ancient Roman republican ideals.

That the American understanding of state both in its general concept and in its particular organs is still strongly shaped by the model of the Roman Republic is not surprising. The thinkers of the French Enlightenment had a strong influence on the leaders of the American struggle for independence from the English crown. The diplomatic and personal ties among representatives of the young American republic and the French state were quite strong. Both Benjamin Franklin and Thomas Jefferson spent several years as envoys in Paris, where they came into contact with the pre-Revolutionary spirit that was consuming all levels of society like a fever.

It is not surprising that Jefferson's 1787 law for the organizing of the Northwest Territory, like his composition of the Declaration of Independence a decade before, was deeply rooted in the ideals of the Roman Republic. Jefferson found the example of Rome a particularly fitting model for the newly annexed agrarian territory. To this day, the United States is formally governed by a Senate housed in the Capitol; the heraldic animal is the bald eagle, an indigenous species, whose iconography nonetheless harkens back to the Roman eagle of Jupiter. Many American coins bear images of the Roman *fasces* (the emblematic bundle of rods carried by the lictors), or symbols of lightning— images also derived from ancient Rome.

Buildings and pictures from the years of revolution and liberation support the political and legal recourse to Roman antiquity on both sides of the Atlantic (**203**). Since the middle of the 18th century, French painting was full of

203 Plaster model of the State Capitol in Richmond, Virginia, built in 1785–89 as a copy of the Roman podium temple, in Nîmes, France. The Capitol was designed by Thomas Jefferson while he was in France. Jefferson sent the model along with the layout and profile back to Virginia while he stayed on in Paris.

5th century – today

historical and mythological themes from the early Roman period. The art was embued with a modern heroic and revolutionary impetus and thus became models of political and social principles of action. Paintings like the *Oath of the Horatii* by Jacques Louis David (**197**) were the talk of the town when they appeared in Parisian salons—sometimes even before their public unveiling, when they were completed in the artist's studio.

The French Baroque had already set its sights on classical Roman models. This Roman emphasis, as opposed to the more sporadic use of ancient Greek building motifs, also dominated late 18th-century French classicism. This was most likely due to the accessibility of ancient Roman structures in southern France, in cities such as Arles, Orange, and Nîmes. Patterns of Roman architecture were available within France itself and constituted an important part of the French national identity.

That buildings of Rome's imperial period, rather than its republican era, became models for 18th- and 19th-century design probably has more to do with the fact that the architecture from the later period survived, while, even in Italy, that of the republican era scarcely exists as ruins. Imperial architecture was familiar in minute detail thanks to the volume of published

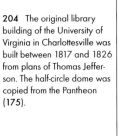

204 The original library building of the University of Virginia in Charlottesville was built between 1817 and 1826 from plans of Thomas Jefferson. The half-circle dome was copied from the Pantheon (**175**).

drawings and sketches. Thus, in France, as in Rome under Augustus, it became possible for a republican dream that ended bloodily as a monarchy to disguise its architectural image in the form of the continuation of the republic, as demonstrated by the imperial gesture of the Napoleonic Arc de Triomphe and other monuments of victories throughout the country.

Classical American architecture of the late 18th and 19th centuries is often designated "Greek Revival," which obviously suggests it is dominated by the classical style from ancient Greece. This American architecture, however, is actually a mixture of elements from both the Greek and the Roman antique periods, as well as from the Renaissance and French classicism. This school of classicism found its ideological and aesthetic champion in Thomas Jefferson. Jefferson was not only a statesman and agrarian economist; he was also an architect who took it upon himself to give the new country its architectural character. His years in France familiarized him with many architects and their buildings, as well as with the ancient Roman ruins of Provence. Jefferson carried all these images and influences back to his home in Virginia and went on to develop an architectural design that fused elements of ancient Rome—such as certain Corinthian columns and forms of entablature, the style of the Roman podium support, and the half-round dome of the Pantheon—with forms borrowed from French classicism. With such elements in mind, he programmatically designed his own estate in Monticello and the overall plan and many of the specific buildings of the University of Virginia in neighboring

205 The Capitol in Washington, D.C., built in three phases between 1793 and 1864, combines architectural elements of ancient Rome, the Renaissance, and French classicism.

5th century – today

5th century – today

206 *Return of the Germans from the Battle of the Teutoburg Forest*, wood engraving based on a painting by Paul Thumann, 1890. Illustrations such as these created an archetypal Germanic hero Hermann based upon the Cheruski tribal chief Arminius. Berlin, Collection of the Prussian Cultural Property.

Charlottesville (**204**). The capitol designed by Jefferson in Richmond, Virginia, is almost an exact copy of the famous Roman podium temple in Nimes in southern France. For the construction of this first public American state building, Jefferson, still a guest in France at the time, sent a plaster model (**203**) and the architectural drawings across the Atlantic by courier. The Capitol Building in Washington, DC (**205**) was begun under Jefferson's political authority, though he was not directly involved in the architectural design; its construction was carried out in stages and it turned into a massive architectural conglomerate of a variety of stylistic elements. This eclecticism became a trademark of American architecture—it is in fact omnipresent in the government buildings in Washington—and in the case of ancient Roman forms, has become an ever recurring theme that still holds some appeal today.

207 Siegfried as prototypical German: This self-made view of the superior Germans was projected back into antiquity. Scene from the 1924 Fritz Lang film *Siegfried*.

Ancient Rome and the Wilhelmine idea of the "German"

The place of Roman classicism in the German Reich of 1871 – 1914 and in the years immediately preceding its foundation suggests a complex scenario in which the ancient world as a whole is accepted as a humanistic model, but is also interpreted in a negative manner in some respects. This apparent contradiction was combined with ideas of "Germanness" and "Nation" to form a compact ideological unit. The antique aesthetic that became a norm of the time owed much to ancient Greece. Greek architecture, sculpture, and philosophy were the backbone of the aesthetic ideal. The material remains of ancient Rome were increasingly relegated to second place. Against this background arose the negative image of Roman culture as a decadent, second-rate epoch of decline within a western civilization that had reached its peak with the Greek classic—an image that has already been discussed in this book.

At the same time, Roman antiquity remained a significant factor in the cultural self-image of the German nation, originally as a foil for the definition of what it meant to be "German." Both national history and national identity were projected back into the ancient classic world; in this idealized imagination, contemporary Germany was identified with the Germanic tribes. Roman texts like Tacitus's *Germania* and Caesar's *bellum gallicum* became the unwitting witnesses of such historical falsification, even of the first obsessive fable spinning about an Aryan-Germanic race. Ideologues like the son-in-law of Richard Wagner, the naturalized German Houston Stewart Chamberlain, whose 1899 *Principles of the Nineteenth Century* also invoked Tacitus in developing his pre-fascist, anti-Semitic racial theory, as had Count Gabineau in his "Essay on the Inequality of the Human Races" (1853–1855). Chamberlain became an exponent of a

208 The reverse side of the 1000-Reichsmark bill from 1910 turned to imperial Rome for its imagery. Personification of districts and virtues was popular on ancient Roman coins and reliefs.

"blood-and-soil" (*Blut-und-Boden*) mythos in which ancient Germanic elements were smelted together with the "Nordic" saga cycle.

Against this background, the resounding victory of the Cheruskian prince Arminius over the legions of Varus near the Teutoburger Forest in the year 9 AD was interpreted as a pinnacle of German history. Arminius, who was raised in Rome and was a knight of the empire, was now dubbed Hermann, the liberator of the Germans. In several late 19th-century paintings and drawings reconstructing the battle (**206**), Hermann was stylized into a victorious hero, and immortalized in an enormous memorial at the presumed site of the battle.

At the same time, however—and this is what blurs the picture—Roman antiquity was also treated as an ideal. The German kaisers saw themselves as following directly in the tradition of the ancient emperors. The numerous representations of German kaisers as knights were borrowed with this idea in mind from the tried-and-true ancient image of the ruler—as in the famous bronze statue of Marcus Aurelius in Rome. Also, the innumerable monuments of these decades, particularly after the German unification of 1871, contained carefully thought-out allusions to imperial Roman art. The allegorical symbolism of the Wilhelmine empire also employed antique pictorial formulas in figures such as "Germania" in everything from ordinary postage stamps to a monumental statue of

209 Bronze, 36 feet high on an 82-foot-high pedestal, looking triumphantly westward: The Germania of the Niederwald National Monument near Rüdesheim. Built in 1877–83 by J. Schilling, the statue borrows its style, allegory, and motifs from ancient Roman imagery.

Germania in triumph over France which was raised on an elevated pedestal near Rüdesheim in 1883 (**209**). Her image is utterly in the tradition of Roman personification of districts and virtues, found in endless repetition on Roman coins and state reliefs from imperial Rome.

Above all, ancient Rome was seen as existing inside Germany. In this respect, the two conflicting perceptions of Roman antiquity—Rome as a model for the state via its symbols and mythos, and Rome as the opponent of the "Germans"—flow irrationally together into an image that was strengthened by popular novels such as Felix Dahn's 1878 *Ein Kampf um Rom* (A Battle for Rome). Late 19th-century scientific and technological refinements allowed for excavation of the many archaeological sites left behind after centuries of Roman occupation of the area from the Rhine to the Danube. Among the greatest finds of the time were the remains of the forts along the *limes*, which in turn provided many examples of the highly developed Roman military technology, an archaeological booty that was entirely in keeping with the martial attitude of the time. It is not surprising that the Saalburg, a Roman fort near Bad Homburg, was rebuilt by kaiser's decree, and turned into an open-air museum between 1898 and 1907. Masses of military paraphernalia from life in the legions were reconstructed here.

Between 1870 and 1900, interest in researching Roman connections with Germany grew from a hobby for interested amateurs into a specialized field among historians studying Germany as a Roman province. Clubs for appreciation of ancient culture, scholarly societies, and state organizations like the Limes Commission of the Reich arose from a framework that contributed to a specious German identity consisting of a complex concoction of racist German ideology and

210 Professional conversation: The German archaeologist Theodor Wiegand (1864–1936) and Emperor Wilhelm II (1859–1941) in Istanbul. The German emperor was an enthusiastic archaeologist and penned several articles on the subject, including his "Memories of Corfu" and the "Studies on Gorgo" (printed while the ruler was in exile between 1924 and 1936).

5th century – today

Roman achievements in technology and civilization—a conception that would later culminate in the racial delusions of National Socialism.

The ancient, the modern, and dictatorship: The role of Roman antiquity in Fascism and Nazism

The European dictators of the 20th century found in the imperial elements of ancient Rome ideal referents for their use of power, as well as ideal patterns for architectural and pictorial articulation of that power. It must have seemed like a cosmic gift from heaven to Benito Mussolini, who had been dictator of Italy with almost unlimited power since the Fascist coup of 1925, that September 29, 1937 was Augustus's 2,000th birthday. Years before, Mussolini had begun elaborate preparations for a celebration several weeks long to mark the occasion. The splendor of the historic greatness of the occasion seemed the best way to unite a split nation, and to present himself as a tradition-conscious *imperator* who would lead his state and his society into a new golden age (**211**).

Toward these ends, massive excavations were begun throughout Italy and the militarily occupied regions of Africa and the Balkans. We should not forget that the Italian state did not pursue this work out of pure motives of selfless research, but largely for political and ideological ulterior motives. Roman antiquity grew out of the earth as if filmed in fast

211 Benito Mussolini reviewing the troops on the newly built avenue before the ancient backdrop. Cover of the weekly paper *Domenica del Corriere*, June 4–10, 1939.

motion. As a stone reminder of historical continuity, the buildings legitimized Italy's claims in North Africa and at the same time provided a grandiose backdrop for the playing out of Fascist power scenarios.

Half of Rome was rebuilt. A splendid wide avenue cut its way like an arrow through Rome's hilly center to connect the Piazza Venezia and the Colosseum. The ancient imperial forums that came to the light of day along this axis formed an effective façade for pompous Fascist parades and drew a direct connection between Mussolini and the "great" rulers—Caesar, Augustus, Trajan—who were the original architects of the buildings and grounds. Plans to construct a "Foro Fascista," a "Mussolini Forum," in the ruins remained unfulfilled. On the dedication of the excavated Caesar's forum, the Roman monthly magazine *Capitolium* wrote in April 1933: "And now lift your spirits! Rome has once more regained one of its most sublime monuments, perhaps the most sublime of all, because it bears the name of Julius Caesar, the greatest man of the Latin world, the most perfect personification of Roman-ness. Born in Rome, of Roman blood—more than a human being. ... And on this day Benito Mussolini stood long before the statue of Caesar and greeted it in the Roman fashion."

Status symbols such as the eagle of the Roman legion enjoyed a sort of a renaissance, as did ancient expressions. In imitation of the

212 Apartment building built in the 1920s on Via Sannio, Rome. The architectural models were the ancient apartment buildings in Ostia (**80, 81**).

Latin *mare nostrum*, the Mediterranean became again the *Mare Nostro*, and many places were given back their ancient names. Another gift from heaven was the Ara Pacis, the great Augustan altar of peace (**64**), which had been rediscovered in the course of construction work, exhumed, and re-erected near the mausoleum of Augustus on the banks of the Tiber. The crowning point of the second millennium festival was an internationally acclaimed exhibition that celebrated the Augustan epoch—but also the "new Rome" of Mussolini.

The exploitation of ancient Rome by Fascist Italy was not limited to such theatrical stagings of surviving, newly excavated, reformed, or restored monuments. Contemporary architecture also was linked with the ancient. In Rome, apartment buildings (**212**) imitated the antique multistory houses in Ostia (see pp. 64–66). For the planned World Exhibition of 1942—

213 The buildings on the grounds of the 1924 World's Fair outside of Rome made numerous references to ancient Roman architecture and city planning. The focal point of the complex today is the Museo della Civiltà Romana, containing the land model of ancient Rome.

"The Roman empire is resurrected
The hour of the eagle has come
The blaring of trumpets accompany its
    flight
From the Capitol to the Quirinal Hill
Earth, we want to rule over you
Sea, we want to sail you
The sign of the lictorate returns
As a symbol of power and civilization"
        "March of the Legions«, 1926. Text by
            Vittorio Bravetta, dedicated to
    "Benito Mussolini, the standard bearer of Rome"

though the exhibition never came about—a modern architecture complex was built between Rome and Ostia to resemble the ancient imperial forums in Rome in both its overall layout and its individual architecture.

The extent to which these modern buildings and their placement can be regarded as truly "ancient" is indicated by how often they have served as settings for historical movies on ancient themes. What was completely unique to this period was the synthesis of the classical modern style (which actually categorically rejected the antique as an ideal) and the architectural images of ancient Rome as realized in the circle gathered around Giuseppe Terragni in "Gruppo 7": The "Casa del Fascio" in Como, for example, was built in 1932–36 as the headquarters of the Fascist party in the form of a transparent cube; its Bauhaus design was based on an ancient architectural concept bolstered by a number of tracts from Vitruvius and his ideals of *firmitas*, *utilitas* and *venustas* (durability, utility, and grace). The architects tried to modernize and to breathe life into these key criteria (**214**).

214 The Casa del Fascio, headquarters of the Fascist Party in Como, was supposed to be an example of the transmission of ancient building forms into modern architectural ideas. The placement of the building opposite the Baroque cathedral made an effective contrast between old and new.

Ancient Rome completely dominated all areas of life in Fascist Italy. National Socialism (Nazism) in Germany, on the other hand, was marked, with the exception of the usurpation of the Roman eagle as a symbol of state, by a complex mixture of Germanic-Nordic mythology and ancient Greek pictorial and architectural forms that were all linked to a crude web of Aryan "Elite Culture," only a small

5th century – today

part of which harkened back to Roman antiquity. In imitation of both ancient and modern monarchical models, the course of the avenue Unter den Linden in Berlin was supposed to be expanded to a large north-south axis. The "Hall of the People," a huge domed building that looks like the Roman Pantheon—the dome would be 460 feet in diameter, over 720 feet high, and the hall would accommodate almost 200,000 spectators—was supposed to be linked above the avenue with a similarly gigantic triumphal arch that would span over the Brandenburg Gate. These lofty ambitions remained just that—ambitions unrealized. Only the model made

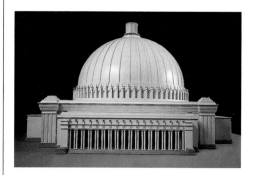

215 The "Great Hall of the People" was supposed to be built in Berlin. Model by the architect Albert Speer, 1936–38.

by Albert Speer (**215**) and Hitler's own sketches of the triumphal arch (**216**) have survived.

In addition to such "Roman" building projects, the Roman relics on German terrain were treated as very important. Just as during the imperial period, so under the Nazis, Roman artifacts remained a local historical component of an artificial national identity that whitewashed the contradictions between the Romans and the German tribes. The excavations at Carnuntum, the "Pompeii by the city gates of Vienna," near Petronell on the Danube were continued after the union between Germany and Austria in 1938. To solicit the necessary funding, the project leader presented Hitler with a deluxe volume on the prior work at the site with the following dedication: "Mein Führer, in the eastern Niederdonau, the remains of the mighty Roman city of Carnuntum still lie today buried in the earth. Two hundred years of war and peace between Germans and Romans had led even in those days to an exchange of cultural goods between these two great peoples, who have now for all time been welded together in the Rome-Berlin Axis. The raising of these treasures ... would be a work worthy of the German nation whose *Lebens-*

216 A triumphal arch in the ancient Roman style was designed to bridge over the Brandenburg Gate in Berlin. Sketch by Adolf Hitler.

raum boasts no other similar memorial. Mein Führer, the decision remains yours." Hitler's response was immediate and positive: "With the reliable sharp eye of the artist, Adolf Hitler at once recognized the immense problem of re-searching the site where at one time Germans and Romans not only measured their strength against each other in heroic battle, but also brought the creative values of their spirits more closely together in peaceful games. And the Führer gave the order: 'Carnuntum shall be ex-cavated!'" (quoted in F. Kreuz, *Rätsel um Carnuntum* [Riddle of Carnuntum], 1939, pp. 58–59).

5th century – today

1430	First mention of the Torso of Belvedere
ca. 1480	Discovery of Hadrian's villa near Tivoli; many statues brought to Rome
1506	"Laokoon" found in Rome. Statuary court set up in the Vatican under Pope Julius II
1538	Michelangelo has the bronze statue of Marcus Aurelius on horseback removed from the Lateran and placed in the Capitol piazza in Rome
1531	Discovery of a Roman ship in Lake Nemi; first attempts at recovery using diving gear (after further failures, actual recovery of vessel in 1928)
1592	First discoveries in the area of Pompeii (tunneling of Domenico Fontana)
1711	Statues uncovered from the theater in Herculaneum
1738-66	Bourbon excavations in Herculaneum
1739	Discovery of Roman Aquileia; systematic excavations since 1872
1748	Beginning of excavations at Pompeii
since 1760	Excavations by English envoy William Hamilton in various necropolises near Naples; first large find of Greek vases

To devote a separate chapter to aspects of the history of discovery and research is consistent with conventions in the modern study of ancient Rome. Yet, it is not really possible to divide a consideration of what we have called the "after-life" of Rome into a history of the influence and interpretation of the ancient Roman world, on the one hand, and a history of scholarship on the other. Scholarship about the ancient world is itself one facet of the overall effect of the ancient world on the modern. It cannot really be studied systematically and scientifically outside the context of its very subject. Nonetheless, for the sake of clarity and simplicity, we will follow convention and survey Roman scholarship in the scope of this final chapter.

The transmission of the ancient Roman world

The history of the transmission of knowledge and traditions about ancient Rome differs radically from that of ancient Greece. After the Ottoman conquest of the Byzantine empire, Greece and its long past were cast aside, to wallow on the sidelines of western history. Of course, the literary achievements of Greece were appreciated, but the physical remains were virtually forgotten and untouched, leaving little scope for centuries for an appreciation of the breadth of Greek art and culture. Rome, on the other hand, never entirely disappeared; its buildings and monuments stood in plain view through the centuries. Even when contemporary attitudes to these remains were decidedly pragmatic (see p. 130ff), ancient Roman sculpture and painting were subjected in the early Renaissance to an ineffable process of artistic idealization that found in them timelessly valid aesthetic principles.

This early artistic attention came hand in hand with the first research and excavation work, although the latter was still a matter more of chance than intention. New construction projects carried out in Rome often unearthed the remains of old buildings and sculpture. This is exactly how the remains of Nero's palace, which in fact had been torn down in the 1st century AD were found in the late 15th century, near the Colosseum. Its wall paintings were widely imitated in the Italian Renaissance, and statues like the Torso of Belvedere, Apollo Belvedere, and the Laokoon, all of which were discovered around 1500 in Rome, prompted Pope Julius II to establish the first museum rooms in the Vatican; such pieces came to stand among the most celebrated art works of antiquity.

The 18th-century rediscovery of Greek culture, unfolding suddenly against the background of the European Enlightenment and improved access to the Balkan lands, had a long-lasting effect on attitudes toward Roman art. Greek masterpieces, already known from Roman writings on ancient art such as Pliny's *naturalis historia*, instantly became foci of artistic interest. In this quest after Greek art, Roman sculpture was increasingly seen as a mere imitation of the "real" classic art. More and more pieces of Roman sculpture were demonstrated to be copies of Greek originals. The writings of Johann Joachim

220 On Wednesday, January 13, 1506, workers digging in a vineyard near the ruins of the Titus baths in Rome came upon "a wonderful marble statue six ells deep in an underground arch": the *Laokoon*. Photo of the most recent and correct reconstruction of 1960. The crooked arm was not discovered until 1905.

1827–44	Discovery of Etruscan necropolises of Tarquinia, Vulci, Cerveteri, and Chiusi; discovery of Etruscan culture
1831	Alexander mosaic discovered in Pompeii
1859	Discovery of the Calixtus catacomb in Rome
1861-69	Uncovering of the emperors' palaces on the Palatine in Rome
1863	Statue of the Primaporta Augustus found near Rome
since 1877	Excavations in Trier
1884	Bronze statues of the Boxer and the Master of the Baths found; today in the Museo Nazionale delle Terme in Rome
1885–1903	Excavations in Kempten
1892–1902	Systematic research of the *limes* by the German Imperial Limes Commission
1899–1904	Excavation of the Roman military camp near Haltern; first observation and interpretations of earth discolorations as remains of posts and palisades
1905	Beginning of excavations of the military camp Vetera near Xanten; since 1934, excavations at Colonia Ulpia Traiana
since 1908	Excavations in Ostia, near Rome

15th century – today

Winckelmann (1717–68), as well as those of Lessing, Herder, and Goethe on ancient classical art cemented this pejorative view of Roman art as nothing more than an aid toward experiencing the more highly prized Greek art. If we think today of Roman art as unoriginal, second-rate, and a mere surrogate, we have this period to thank for our biases.

Very important in the handing down of Roman antiquity were the investigations of Roman buildings, which often led to lavish folios and other publications of design specifications—mass, proportion, volume, dimensions—with detailed drawings, architectural sketches, and reconstructions. Such publications highlight the close connection between the history of scientific research and the history of the perceptions of ancient Rome. Research efforts directed at Roman architecture grew wholly out of a desire to study the forms and techniques of ancient architecture and to replicate it in new architectural relationships. In other words, a nonscientific concern became the driving force behind scientific interest. Palladio's *Book on the Antiquities of Rome*, written in 1554, was a milestone of architectural knowledge of the Roman past. Later, Antoine Desgodetz's 1682 publication on ancient Roman buildings, along with reports and drawings from English expeditions to the ruins of Palmyra (1753) and Baalbek (1757),

221 Arch in the loggias in the Villa Madama in Rome, decorated in 1500 with ornamental grotesques copied from paintings in the house of Nero which had been recently discovered.

15th century – today

160

provided such exact architectural detail that it became possible to replicate the buildings on other locations.

The many discoveries since 1800, especially in Greece, constantly fueled research and filled the store rooms of ancient and antiquarian collections. There was a demand to know ever more about the ancient classical world, and this demand was fed by increasing specialization in areas of science such as philology, archaeology, and the study of inscriptions. The interest in Greece still dominated, but Rome remained the organizational center of classical studies—if for no other reason than that its infrastructure was more accessible and its artifacts nearer at hand. The German Archaeological Institute, established in 1823 out of a private society, was officially sanctioned by the Prussian state in 1857. Among its missions and obligations, it was also to maintain a certain diplomatic function. Its overriding goal was to assemble, organize, catalog, and publish an archive of ancient Greek and Roman monuments.

Since that time, perceptions of ancient Rome have been expanded and refined by the proliferation of excavations. These were, however, until recently confined to digs whose express purpose was to look for the old "Roman" world; excavations were confined to sites in Italy and in the provinces once under direct Roman control. The approach toward areas historically "Greek" in origin was quite another matter. Like the Roman sites, promising sites for Greek research continued to be inhabited well into the Roman and Byzantine periods. By the time archaeologists set out to unearth them, they had been covered over with the

EXCAVATING NEAR THE TEMPLE OF JUPITER, STATOR. ROME.

222 Excavations in Rome at the temple of Castor: Three-foot layers of earth and debris caused by flooding and erosion first had to be cleared away to reach the ancient ground level.

223 Drawing of a capital from the Roman Pantheon from Antoine Desgodetz's "Edifices antiques de Roma" of 1682. Such precise drawings were the basis of imitations of ancient architecture since the late 17th century.

15th century – today

massive layers of detritus of the succeeding eras and cultures. Unfortunately, many projects proceeded with a kind of single-mindedness of purpose—so focused on the search for Greek artifacts that they overlooked the layers of potentially illuminating materials under which their prize was buried. Much that might have dramatically helped flesh out our picture of Roman and Byzantine life was often summarily dismissed with perfunctory and sloppy documentation, or flat-out discarded. What specific knowledge we have available today about the "Roman" history of a "Greek" shrine like Olympia is mainly thanks to very recent research.

The excavation of a culture: The discoveries of Pompeii and Herculaneum

Much of what we know about ancient Rome and Roman culture we learned from the excavations of Pompeii and Herculaneum. Pompeii, just south of Naples on the slopes of Mount Vesuvius, and Herculaneum, five miles to the east, were buried when Vesuvius erupted in 79 AD. Until the discovery and excavation of these cities, knowledge of Roman antiquity had been a patchwork affair, pasted together with bits of information garnered by chance with unclear or unknown interconnection. The loss of Pompeii and of Herculaneum (and of several smaller villages within the vicinity of the volcano) was the scholar's fortune in time. Sculptures, coins, jewelry, with their artistic character and portability, were the first boons to emerge from the ancient devastation. When the excavations really got underway, however, what emerged from under the three-foot-thick layers of lava and ash would stun the world, for it was beyond anything ever unearthed in recent memory. Here was a complete world that had been buried instantaneously—moved in a flash, so to speak, from life to death. Preserved by

224 Charles of Bourbon, who ruled Naples between 1734 and 1759, supported the excavations at Herculaneum and Pompeii for the sake of his own dominion. Painting by Francisco Goya. Madrid, Prado.

15th century – today

the very means that had destroyed their lives, the inhabitants of these cities survived as a "frozen" slice of Roman daily life. Pompeii and Herculaneum did not offer the world riches; it was not art that was uncovered here (even if that was what the project leaders hoped to find). In these digs the archaeologists found instead the remains of the ancient classic life in its infinite variety and heretofore unmeasured entirety. Once again, the ancient world was idealized: Every new announcement of finds from the two cities inspired some new fashion. Whether ornaments, wall paintings, mosaic motifs, or the decoration of vessels and containers, many of the patterns were greedily adopted by the commercial art manufacturers of the 18th and 19th centuries.

The excavations of the cities buried by Vesuvius had actually begun not long after the smoke from the eruption cleared. Refugees from the disaster returned to their homes to try to retrieve their buried belongings. An imperial commission protected the survivors from plunderers and offered them assistance to dig tunnels for the recovery of victims and belongings. Despite efforts to forestall looting, there was large-scale marauding. In 1592, when the architect Domenico Fontana dug a tunnel straight under Pompeii to lay a water main, the ancient natural catastrophe and its precise location were little more than

225 Excavated area in Herculaneum as a tourist attraction, ca. 1810. Etching by François Benoist.

15th century – today

163

226 Excavated area in Pompeii as a tourist attraction in 1810: Noble visitors in the House of the Tragic Poet. Watercolor by François Benoist.

a vague memory. But in the course of Fontana's work, as well as later ditch-digging projects in the 17th century, objects and even inscriptions turned up, though no one seemed terribly impressed and no further systematic research was undertaken.

It took another accident to ignite the chain of real excavations. In 1711, during construction of the Bourbon palace at Portici near Naples, sculptures and architectural remains of the theater of ancient Herculaneum were uncovered. Comprehensive excavations were finally undertaken at the site between 1738 and 1766 and, following more chance discoveries, also in Pompeii starting in 1748 (although Pompeii was thought at the time to be the buried city of Stabiae). These Bourbon excavations were not, as archaeologist Agnes Allrogen-Bedel convincingly explains, a scientific endeavor but merely a self-aggrandizing action of royal and courtly display—the excavation work was driven by the desire to find, recover, restore, document, and show off in museums whatever might be there to be recovered and so handled. Archaeology, in this context, was a political action of the state, carried out by officials of the court, not by scientists at all. The digging was carried on under strict secrecy and in the face of certain dangers. Pockets of methane gas and the repeated collapse of poorly shored-up tunnels sometimes turned the excavations at Herculaneum into a fatal adventure.

Everything that could possibly be moved was taken from the site and brought to the specially built Museo Ercolanese at Portici; whatever could not be removed was sometimes deliberately destroyed in a true spoilsport gesture—so that it would not fall into anyone else's hands. Until the findings were published, they were shown only to a small, selected audience of non-specialists; when they were published, they were released in the form of the elaborately produced, but already scientifically outdated deluxe edition of the *Antichità de Ercolaneo* (8 volumes, 1757–92). Museum visitors were not allowed to either write or draw but were literally driven through the museum in small groups so that they could not get a closer impression of any unpublished objects. Even under these restrictions, which did not sit well with public figures such as German poet and essayist Johann Wolfgang von Goethe or German archaeologist Johann Winckelmann and others, many visitors still managed to produce remarkably exact drawings of individual pieces from memory.

In 1766 the excavations of Herculaneum were abandoned in favor of Pompeii, which, unlike Herculaneum, was covered by a relatively thin layer of ashes buried under a three-foot-thick layer of lava. Large-surface excavations, which soon became a popular attraction, were begun between 1806 and 1815. Excavation became a popular entertainment: "discoveries" were staged for prominent guests by burying certain objects shortly before the visitors' arrival, and then uncovering them "by chance" while the visitors watched.

With the appointment of Giuseppe Fiorelli as director of the excavations, the project was placed on a scientific footing. Fiorelli divided the city of Pompeii into regions, *insulae* (blocks), a scheme still used today. He conceived of Pompeii as an open-air museum and, where possible, left the findings in place; he even tried to

227 Plaster corpses: Casts of victims of Vesuvius in the positions in they were found.

15th century – today

Johann Caspar Goethe, father of Johann Wolfgang von Goethe, describing his visit to the Museo Ercolanese in Portici:

"Even before the present king ascended the throne, discoveries had been made and many articles found; since he has become king, however, dedicated research throughout the entire city of Herculaneum has turned up many rare and valuable objects that are now installed and kept in the great hall in Portici. One can view them there but is not allowed to make any drawings because the king or the minister wants to keep the fame for himself ... or to have engravings made of them which he may present to the public and to the scholarly world." (Letter of April 10, 1740)

re-create the gardens of individual houses. Only especially valuable objects or those that could be sensitive to exposure to the elements were brought to the new national museum in Naples.

Now at last state-of-the-art excavation techniques were used. For example, Fiorelli oversaw the first experiments with making poured plaster casts of the spaces left by objects, or bodies, that had decayed and left behind empty forms in the ground. The plaster forms of the dead made in 1863 were spectacular—inconspicuous hollow spaces in the lava were transformed into casts of people frozen in the moment of death. And close observation could reveal the smallest details of daily life—the remains of a small basket of bread; charred beans and onions in a kitchen.

Between 1860 and 1940 Pompeii was extensively excavated—which may or may not please a visitor today. Of course, it was only by laying open such broad areas that one could experience the density of the population, the infrastructure, and the public, economic, and private life of an ancient Roman city. But preservation of historical monuments is still problematic; for example, the rubble of almost 100 years of digging lay in large piles strewn over the land, making further work impossible. In weary efforts stretching over years, the rubble was cleared away by 1954. Still, far too little money is available to finance the constant restoration work, to pay for guards, to hire gardeners to keep the vegetation appropriately pruned, so that the city, now excavated but still partially closed to the public, is in the throes of a second downfall (albeit a somewhat less violent one). Fortunately, some unexcavated areas remain and at least a small part of Pompeii will be around for the pleasure and enlightenment of future generations.

15th century – today

Between progress and fantasy: Experimental archaeology

Ancient Rome has often been looked at through the lens of a new archaeological approach aimed at reconstructing the past as completely and authentically as possible. Only in this way, proponents of such a view maintain, can we arrive at a full imaginative appreciation of these segments of the past. The techniques used by such "experimental archaeology" were originally developed in the context of the practically oriented students of pre-history; it was only a matter of time before they were applied to the study of the ancient Roman period as well. Such an approach has always attracted a good deal of attention and has in fact often prompted—beyond its immediate spectacular effect—important hypotheses concerning the ancient classical world.

"Experimental archaeology" has long roots, reaching back into the medieval and early modern periods when extensive attempts were made to re-create ancient Roman technology. Building and engineering methods for the construction of aqueducts and bridges tended to attract most scholars' attention, with agricultural and mining techniques cropping up in the works of Cato, Columella and Agricola. The aim of these so-called experiments was to realize certain practical improvements in contemporary technology through efforts to understand the technology of the past, and to assess its current utility. It is only in recent decades that historical simulation and reconstruction have been pursued for the sake of science alone. The numerous discoveries concerning daily Roman life yielded up by the cities buried under Vesuvius ash and in the extremely carefully excavated military camps north of the Alps have provided fertile ground for research. A prime area for experimental archaeological simulation has been the military. Back in the

228 1st-century AD Roman horse soldier, dressed for battle. Reconstruction.

15th century – today

19th century, attempts were made to reconstruct ancient weapons to determine their accuracy and force. Archaeologist Marcus Junkelmann's spectacular series of experiments replicated many aspects of the life of the Roman legionnaires, including battle techniques and tactics, speed of march, style of riding, and details of the equipment.

The truth is that much of ancient Roman technology can only be understood through experiment. One salient example is the complicated shelving and ventilation systems used by pottery works in loading the kilns, as well as for the actual firing of the brick-red Terra Sigillata (107).

Some researchers have made efforts to reproduce authentic Roman cuisine. They have tested mills and studied the functioning of ancient ovens. By a combination of surviving ancient Roman recipes and archaeological findings, there have been attempts—sometimes even with commercial motives—to make ancient Roman food palatable to modern taste—even that trademark of Roman cookery, the ubiquitous *garum*, a hot, putrid, fermented fish-based sauce poured over all dishes. The tavern in the hostel at the Archaeological Park Xanten serves Roman meals upon request (modified, though, to suit modern taste).

Many ancient reconstructions created in recent years are not—or are only to a small extent—the product of an experimental simulation for the sake of better understanding. More often, such activity represents the attempt to offer the modern visitor a model of the ancient world—whether it is something they can walk through, touch, smell, or taste. But the objectivity

229 Reconstructed antiquity: The Burginatium Gate in the Archaeological Park at Xanten.

15th century – today

inherent in experimental archaeology as a method of trial-and-error can sometimes run amuck. The result may be that archaeological parks such as Xanten or Kempten with their partial or complete reconstructions really only offer preserved specimens whose artificial fossilization build a picture of architectural history as a static condition, rather than as what it was—a dynamic cycle of construction, maintenance, reconstruction, and decay.

230 Food in ancient Rome: Reconstructed dining room in the hostel at the Archaeological Park, Xanten.

In lieu of conclusion: Ancient Rome from the perspective of contemporary ancient studies

Ancient Rome and ancient studies—an unhappy love affair that has lasted for many years—have not yet found a way to live happily ever after. Even if justice has been done to ancient Rome in the area of excavations, and its equal ranking with other ancient cultures and eras has been established; even if Rome is in many respects an important subject of research in ancient history and the breadth of its cultural history is on display in the museums of the world, a virulent remnant of its old, negative image nonetheless remains, however subtly, in the present day.

Since the late 1960s, imperial Roman art has been of particular interest to archaeologists. Instead of enjoying the luxury of thoughtfully observing art from an ivory tower—a scholastic stance that peaked in the 1950s—students of history, or art, or archaeology must leave their towers and address the "social relevance" of art. As welcome as this change in the understanding of the subject is—it seems particularly necessary today to embue ancient studies, that is, "classics," with a profound sense of relevance

15th century – today

169

to our own world—we must not overlook the possibility that the result of this drive for relevance has also contributed to the trivialization of efforts to understand ancient Rome.

If art was once a political medium in the form of a display of dominance, the state art of imperial Rome seemed to some historians to epitomize this idea. That is, in Rome, everything worked together toward a unity of art and power. The archaeologists interpreted the Trajan's arch at Benevent (**231**) with its decorative reliefs as a monument covered with a richly detailed, allusive, allegorical pictorial language, fleshed out with stylistic nuances, plenty of pictorial references to events and connections—in short, as a readable, even graphically demonstrable program of political measures and claims in which the emperor, as supreme ruler, held all the cards. Other examples of the programmatic expression of either the ruling self-image or a bourgeois-aristocratic order (by other patrons) were also seen, according to these archaeologists, in series of statues in villas, and in the magnificent cameos, wall paintings, and entire families of media such as architecture and literature.

Certainly, such views reflect realities of the ancient world and contain a kernel of truth. But the ideal of a "politicized" art of the Roman state or of the upper class is only on the surface the result of surviving old value judgments. From either a sociological or an historical viewpoint, the model of an omnipotent, all-determining emperor is almost painfully simple. More likely, the historical reality was more complex, even in the most totalitarian monarchies (and even there, there was always more than one protagonist and more than one central authority).

Such an understanding of artistic conception is similarly one-sided. The monuments were, as

231 Trajan's Arch in Benevent as a vehicle of the imperial visual program. Sketch by the archaeologist Klaus Fittschen, 1972.

German archaeologist Burkhard Fehr contends, conceived as the message of only the person who commissioned them; little consideration was given to what the audience to whom the message was addressed would understand. It was this attitude that finally defined once more, and decisively, the cardinal difference between Roman and Greek art. According to this view, Roman art was propagandistic art, a profanely political utilitarian art, in contrast to the Greek ideal of art, which was in turn exalted as the sublime emanation of superior spiritual understanding. Concomitantly, all efforts to evaluate Greek art as a medium subject to social processes and pressures were absolutely rejected well into the 1980s.

Thus, the traditional value judgments concerning ancient Rome donned modern clothing and continued to circulate, along with the factually inadequate, but nonetheless persistent— one might say tenacious—comparisons of Roman with Greek culture—a rather sobering balance after thirty years of social orientation within the field of ancient studies.

232 Cologne, Roman-Germanic Museum: The Roman culture on exhibition. In recent years, department stores have adopted the style of museums, while the museums reverse the trend and present objects and reproductions in the style of gift shops.

15th century – today

Glossary

Glossary

Aedicula: Small architectural structure resembling a temple; niche with columns and gabled front.

Aedile: Urban administrative official, responsible for the police, watching over the market, traffic, and grain supply. In Rome, aids to the People's Tribune; see *Tribune*.

Ager publicus: State land (i.e., not in private individual ownership) in Rome and the provinces.

Annals: Official writing of history in ancient Rome.

Auxiliary troops: Support troops of the regular army; usually made up of soldiers without citizenship rights.

Basilica: Public buildings in Rome constructed for mercantile and judicial purposes through private initiative and named after the patron. Later, the basic form of the early Christian churches.

Canabae: Civilian settlements near a military base.

Cardo: X-axis in Roman land surveying; main street in a Roman military camp or in a city; see *Decumanus*.

Censor: Roman official, usually a former consul, responsible for the creation of citizen lists and division of the citizens in the Tribus; office open also to plebeians since 351 BC.

Centuriatio: Roman land surveying.

Chora: Economic and political district surrounding and belonging to a polis.

Clientes: Members of a group protected by a wealthy Roman of the upper class; from Lat. *cluere* = to obey.

Collegium: Usual organizational form of professional societies, or a cult community. Term for a society or union in ancient Rome.

Colonia: City governed by Roman or Latin law, judicially superior to a municipium (see *municipium*).

Comitia: Assembly within the Roman army, or people's assembly.

Consul: Highest magistrate of the Republic; always a pair of officials with equal rights (see *two-man Gremium*); the almost complete list of the consuls is an important aid in dating historical events.

Corona civica: Wreath of the free citizen during the Republican period; later transformed into the sign of monarchy.

Decumanus: Y-axis in Roman land surveying; the street intersecting the cardo in a Roman military base or city.

Decurio: Head of a city council; member of the decurion order (i.e., the 100 wealthiest citizens of a city).

Diocese: Administrative unit in Late Antiquity, superior to the provinces; bishop's district in Christianity.

Duumvirs, or **duumviri:** Collegial two-man team, serving for one year as the highest officials of a city (similar to a modern mayor).

Epigraphics: Science of inscriptions, from Greek *epi grafein* = to write down; special discipline within ancient studies.

Fasces: Bundle of rods with an axe; see *lictor*.

Fasti: Calendar of offices and festivals; list of officials.

Fibula: Ornate clothing pin.

Forma urbis: Large marble city map, publicly erected under Septimius Severus in the Nerva Forum; many fragments remain.

Garum: Sauce made out of spices and fermented fish, served with almost all dishes and traded in large amphoras (a sort of Roman ketchup).

Groma: Surveyor's tool.

Imperator: Emperor, or "proprietor" of the empire; later honorary title for successful generals.

Glossary

Imperium: Authority of command belonging to the highest magistrates; essence of the Roman power system.

Insula: Blocks of houses bordered by streets; also apartment houses with several rental apartments.

Kline: Couch for lying, sleeping, eating, and drinking.

Knight: The *ordo equites*; second highest class in Roman society; see *ordo*.

Lares: Protective gods of the household, family, or fields; mostly worshipped in a *lararium*, shrine, or an *aedicula* in the atrium of the Roman house, but also along field borders and crossroads.

Legate: Envoy and representative of the Roman senate, the emperor's representative in a province (praetor; governor); since the reign of Augustus, also the commander of a legion.

Legion: Army formation; 6,000-man authorized strength since Marius.

Lictor: Beadle of the higher magistrates in Rome; they publicly carried the *fasces* (bundle of rods with an axe) before the officials.

Magistratus: Collective term for public offices and office holders in Rome and Roman cities.

Mos majorum: Lat.: "customs of the ancestors." Traditional practices, providing a weighty moral argument in many circumstances.

Munera: Service or duty rendered by citizens to the state or community; originally voluntary, later forced acceptance of offices, subsidizing of the communities, etc.

Municipium: City with its own administration in contrast to *colonia*, with limited citizenship rights (*cives sine suffragio* = citizens without voting rights).

Nobiles: Members of the nobility.

Nymphaeum: Fountain construction providing water in public and private areas; in the imperial era, it was sometimes fitted with a several-story ornamental façade.

Oppidum: Latin term for Celtic refuge fort; city-like settlement without legal status.

Ordo: Status or group in Roman society; also, determination of heirship rights and general term for corporations (see *decurio*).

Pater familias: Clan head possessing wide legal rights (*patria potestas* = paternal power) but also duties.

Patrician: Derivative of *patres*; members of the gentility/nobility.

Penates: Roman household gods, often associated and/or combined with the *lares*.

Peristyle: Courtyard or room surrounded by columns.

Plebs urbana: Plebeians of the city of Rome; not denigrated to equivalent of "rabble" until after the ancient period.

Plebs, plebeians: The mass of the Roman citizens, as distinct from the patricians.

Podium temple: Roman temple on a high foundation with wide front steps (in contrast to the Greek column temple, open on all sides).

Polis: Autonomous Greek cities since the 7th century BC.

Pomerium: Circle drawn by Romulus in mythological story; later borders of the city of Rome.

Praetor: Highest administrative officials in Rome, directly under the consuls; in other cities, subject to the *duumvirs*.

Proconsul: Governor of a province; see *legate*.

Quaestor: Official responsible for finances in Rome and the provinces.

Senate: Council of the elders (*senes*); heads of the patrician families; highest organ of debate and decision, largely ineffectual

Glossary ... Historical Overview

during the imperial period. The highest *ordo* of the Roman society.

Socii: From *socius*, confederate groups in the Roman league; allies with legally defined rights and duties.

Spolie: Element of older building incorporated into a new one (pillar, column, etc.).

Substruction: Massive podium, the foundation of a Roman building; often seen as a sign of the triumph of culture over nature.

Suburbs: Thickly settled city area containing apartment houses.

Toga: Roman clothing; also status symbol of a free citizen.

Tribune: Roman official; since the 5th century BC, representative of the plebeians with veto right. Insignificant as office from the late republican period, but "tribunal power" remained important to the legitimization of the emperor's power. In the republican army, the six highest officers who alternately held command.

Tropaion: Demonstrative pile of weapons and other war booty erected on the site of a military victory.

Two-man committee: Ancient principle for the prevention of despotism:

important offices and functions were filled and performed by two persons.

Veteran: Retired soldier with a claim on governmental provision.

Vicus: Village, hamlet, town, marketplace, or crossroads settlement without city rights.

Villa: Luxurious country house.

Historical Overview— A Short Survey of the History of Ancient Rome

10th century BC	Earliest remains of Roman settlement
753	Mythical founding of Rome, according to Varro
616–510	Rule by kings in Rome
510–509	Banning of the kings; start of the republican system; beginning of the List of Consuls, Brutus first consul
494	Beginning of class conflict between plebeians and patrician nobility; gradual improvement of legal status of the plebeians (Tribunes of the People)
450	Law of the Twelve Tables. Establishment of the Assembly of the Army, divided into five levels of power (Assembly of the People)
396	Rome conquers Etruscan city of Veii and grows from a city into a territorial state
387	Rome defeated by Celts, city occupied by Celtic troops (*vae victis!* = "Woe to the defeated")
366	Plebeians admitted into Consulate
343–341	First war against the Samnites

Historical Overview

340–338 War against the Latins

326–304 Second war against the Samnites

298–290 Third war against the Samnites, wars against the Etruscans and Celts

287 Lex Hortensia: resolutions of the tribune-led People's Assembly accepted as binding by the patricians; end of class conflict

285–282 War against the Celts and Etruscans

282 Wars against Tarent, King Pyrrhus of Epirus, the Samnites, and the Lucanians

264–241 First Punic War with Carthage; Sicily conquered

225–222 War with the Celts in northern Italy

218–201 Second Punic War with Carthage; Hannibal crosses the Alps (218), wins the battle at Cannae (216), and marches on Rome (<*Hannibal ante portas* = "Hannibal before the gates," 211); Scipio defeats Hannibal as Zama (202–201 BC)

171–168 Third Macedonian war against King Perseus; conquest of Greece following the battle of Pydna (168 BC)

148–146 Revolts in Greece; siege and destruction of Corinth (146 BC)

146 Third Punic War; destruction of Carthage

133 King Attalos of Pergamon bequeaths his kingdom to Rome

107–100 Consulate of Marius; military reform

91–89 Revolt of the Italian confederates (Confederate's War), who afterward receive Roman citizenship

82–79 Dictatorship of Sulla

60 First triumvirate (Pompey, Caesar, Crassus)

58–51 Caesar conquers Gaul

49 Civil war between Caesar and Pompey; Caesar crosses the Rubicon (*alea jacta est* = "the die is cast"). Defeat of Pompey at Pharsalos in central Greece

45 Caesar becomes dictator for life

44 Assassination of Caesar

43–42 Second triumvirate (Mark Antony, Octavian/Augustus, Lepidus); victory over the assassins of Caesar at Philippi

31 Victory of Octavian/Augustus against Mark Antony in the sea battle near Actium

27 Senate grants Octavian the honorary title of Augustus; end of the Republic, beginning of empire

15 Conquest of Raetia and Noricum

12 BC–9 AD Campaigns against the Illians, Pannonnians, and Germans. Defeat of Varus (9 AD), and securing of the Rhine border)

14–68 AD Death of Augustus (14 AD), Julian-Claudian dynasty

43 Conquest of Britain

62 Earthquake in Pompeii

68–69 Year of the four emperors: Galba, Vitellius, Otho, and Vespasian

69 Revolt of the Batavians in Germany; destruction of numerous forts

69–96 Flavian dynasty

70 Conquest and plundering of Jerusalem under Titus

79 Eruption of Vesuvius; destruction of Pompeii, Herculaneum, and Stabiae

83–85 War with Chatti; beginning of construction of the *limes* against the Germans

96–180 Period of adoptive emperors

101–106 Trajan's first and second Dacian wars; establishment of Dacia as province

114–117 Parthian wars; eastern border of the empire set by treaty at the Euphrates

132–135 Jewish uprising

167–180 First and second wars under Marcus Aurelius against the Marcomanni; fortification of the border at the Danube

180–193 Beginning of the period of the soldier-emperors

Historical Overview

193–235 Severine dynasty

212 Roman citizenship granted to all inhabitants of the provinces

235–285 Soldier-emperors; political, military, social, and economic crisis

254 Breakdown of the Rhine-Danube border

259–260 Withdrawal from the upper German-Raetian *limes*

260–273 Splitting of the kingdom of Palmyra under Odainathos and Zenobia

261–274 Special kingdoms of Postumus and Tetricius in Gaul

270–271 Withdrawal from the province of Dacia

284–305 First Tetrarchy (Diocletian, Maximian, Constantius, Galerius); reestablishment of the political and military structures; reform policies

287–294 Special kingdoms of Carausius and Allectus in Britain

305–306 Second Tetrarchy (Constantius, Galerius, Maxentius, Constantine)

311 Edict of Toleration; Christianity becomes a legal religion

312 Victory of Constantine on the Milvian Bridge over Maxentius; Constantine converted to Christianity

324 Constantine overcomes Licinius and rules alone

325 Council of Nicea; Christianity becomes the state religion

330 Festive dedication of Constantinople as new capital city

361–363 Julian the Apostate; attempt to reinstate the pagan cults

375–376 Huns overrun the kingdom of the Ostrogoths

391–392 Ban against pagan worship; first massacres and persecutions of pagans

395 Death of Theodosius; division into an eastern and western Roman empire

401–429 Tribal migrations of West Goths, Alans, Vandals, Suebi, Saxons

402 Western Roman court moved to Ravenna

410 West Goths conquer Rome under Alaric

451–452 Battle of the Catalaunian Fields; Huns invade Italy

455 Vandals plunder Rome

476 Romulus Augustulus deposed as western emperor; end of western Roman empire

482–511 Creation of France under the rule of Chlodwig

488–489 Ostrogoths in Italy

490–493 Battle for Ravenna between Theoderich and Odoakar; assassination of Odoakar

526 Theoderich dies in Ravenna

527–567 Reign of Justinian; attempt to restore the unified Roman empire

529 Justinian closes the Athens Academy; plundering of pagan temples; persecutions of pagans

537 Hagia Sophia dedicated; dome collapses (558)

567 Death of Justinian

Roman Emperors ... Museums and Collections

The Roman Emperors

27 BC–14 AD	Augustus
14–37	Tiberius
37–41	Caligula
41–54	Claudius
54–68	Nero
68–69	Galba, Otho, Vitellius
69–79	Vespasian
79–81	Titus
81–96	Domitian
96–98	Nerva
98–117	Trajan
117–138	Hadrian
138–161	Antoninus Pius
161–180	Marcus Aurelius
180–192	Commodus
193	Pertinax, Didius Julianus
193–197	Clodius Albinus
193–194	Pescennius Niger
193–211	Septimius Severus
198–217	Caracalla
217–218	Macrinus
218–222	Elagabal
222–235	Alexander Severus
235–238	Maximinus Thrax
238	Gordian I, Gordian II, Balbinus, Pupienus
238–244	Gordian III
244–249	Philippus Arabs
249–251	Decius
251	Herennius, Hostilianus
251–253	Trebonianus Gallus, Volusianus
253	Aemilianus
253–260	Valerian
260–261	Ingenuus, Regalianus, Quietus, Macrianus
261–262	Aemilianus
260–268	Gallienus
268–270	Claudius Gothicus
270	Quintillus
270–275	Aurelianus
275–276	Tacitus
276	Florianus
276–282	Probus
282–283	Carus
283–285	Carinus
283–284	Numerian
284–305	Diocletian (1st tetrarchy)
305–306	2nd tetrarchy
306–337	Constantine (single ruler after 324)
337–361	Rule of the sons of Constantine
361–363	Julian ("Apostata")
363–379	Jovian, Valentinian I, Valens, Gratian, Valentinian II
379–395	Theodosius

West Roman emperors

395–423	Honorius
423–425	John
425–455	Valentinian III
457–461	Maiorianus
461–465	Libius Servus
467–472	Anthemius
472	Olybrius
472–474	Glycerius
474–475	Nepos
475–476	Romulus

East Roman emperors

395–408	Arcadius
408–450	Theodosius II
450–457	Marcian
457–474	Leo I
474–491	Zeno
491–518	Anastasius
518–527	Justin I
527–565	Justinian

Museums and Collections of Roman Art and Cultural History

Important Archaeological Excavations

Algeria

Timgad: ancient Thamugadi; well-preserved city from the time of the Roman emperors

Tebessa: ancient Theveste; well-preserved colonial city with buildings from the 2nd and 3rd centuries AD

Austria

Klagenfurt: Landes-museum für Kärnten; collection of regional finds on art and cultural history

Petronell: ancient Carnuntum; reconstructed excavations of the 1930s; small museum

Vienna: Ephesos-Museum; informative documentation of the Austrian excavations in Ephesos with special focus on Roman antiquity

Croatia

Split: ancient Spalato/Salona; the complete old city is built into the palace of Diocletian from the early 4th century AD

Museums and Collections

Denmark:

    Copenhagen: Ny Carlsberg Glyptotek; Roman sculptures, famous collection of Roman portraits

France

    Arles: ancient Arelate; well-preserved amphitheater

    Lyon: Musée de la Civilisation Gallo-Romaine; well-presented cultural historical collection on Gallic and Roman finds

    Nîmes: Museé Archéologique; finds from the Provence; apart from that many spolia from buildings of ancient Nemausus in the nearby area

    Orange: ancient Arausio; well-preserved Roman theater and honorary arch

    Paris: Musée du Louvre; exquisite collection of Roman art

Germany:

    Aalen: Limesmuseum; instructive exhibitions on the Germanic-Raetian *limes*

    Bad Homburg: Saalburgmuseum in reconstructed fort; extensive collection of Roman military material

    Bonn: Rheinisches Landesmuseum; main museum for the finds on the history of the German provinces of Rome in the Rhineland

    Cologne: Römisch-Germanisches Museum; extensive but because of its presentation often criticized exhibition on ancient Roman cultural history with finds from Cologne and its closer surroundings; numerous spolia of ancient builings all over the old city

    Haltern: Römisch-Germanisches Museum; finds and documentation of the history of the excavation of the legionary camp destroyed in 9 AD

    Hannover: Kestner-Museum; well-presented, very extensive collection of Roman coins

    Mainz: Mittelrheinisches Landesmuseum; regional collection of art and cultural history

    Passau: Römermuseum; finds from the Boiotro fort

    Trier: Rheinisches Landesmuseum; regional collection especially on art and cultural history; numerous buildings and spolia from the Roman city Augusta Treverorum, among others the Porta Nigra (3rd century AD)

    Xanten: ancient Colonia Ulpia Traiana; archaeological park with partly reconstructed buildings; museum on the ground of the excavations; in town regional musem with a collection on the history of the city

Great Britain

    Colchester: ancient Camoludunum with an excavated legionary camp and massive city walls

    Fishbourne: Antiquarium; small museum with finds from a well-preserved and excavated Roman villa

    London: British Museum; exquisite pieces on Roman antiquity, among others the "Esquiline Treasure" as well as numerous Roman finds from all over England; unique collection of Roman coins

    Newcastle: Museum of Antiquities; collection of regional finds on art and cultural history

Greece

    Athens: National Museum; complete presentation of the history of ancient Greece and Rome; numerous Roman buildings in the antique part of the city

    Corinth: Archaeological Museum; many finds from the ancient Roman city which had been built on the site of the prior Greek settlement destroyed in 146 BC; excavations since 1950

Philippi: late antique and early byzantine church city with a small museum

Thessalonica: many ruins and spolia of the ancient Roman city (Arch of Galerius, Galerius' palace); important early byzantine church buildings

– Archaeological Museum; good general overview on the late antique Roman phase of settlement

– Museum in the 'White Tower'; collection on the history of the city, especially with finds from byzantine times

– Byzantine National Museum; collection on byzantine history and culture from all over Greece; still in the process of collecting

Italy

Arezzo: Museo Archeologico; extensive collection of the city's Terra Sigillata and well-presented information on the production and distribution of this ceramic

Baiae: spectacular finds of underwater archaeology in the antique spa which

today lies under the sea level; museum with finds from and documentation of the excavations

Capua: remains of the ancient town with well-preserved amphitheater

Ercolano: buildings and ruins of the city of Herculaneum, which was covered by the 79 AD eruption of Vesuvius

Florence: Museo Archeologico and Uffizi; one of the best collections of Roman art

Naples: Museo Archeologico Nazionale; finds from the cities covered during the 79 AD Vesuvius eruption, collection of Greek vases from southern Italy

Ostia: Antiquarium with many finds from the excavations in the former harbor city of Rome

Paestum: Greek city in Campania with famous doric temples; the museum with finds from Paestum concentrates on the history of Greek colonization

Palermo: Museo Archeologico Regionale; main museum for archaeological finds from all over Sicily

Piazza Armerina in Sicily; luxurious villa of the time around

400 AD; many mosaics are still in their original location

Pompeii: city covered during the 79 AD Vesuvius eruption; extensive excavation area

Puteoli: Greek colonial city on the north of the Gulf of Naples; extensive Roman ruins, including an amphitheater

Ravenna: Museo Nazionale; extensive collection of late antique western art under Theoderich; many architectural remainders of this period in the area

Rome: the city is an unparalleled unique free-light museum of ancient Roman architecture and urbanism

– Musei Capitolini; Palazzo dei Conservatori; Museo Nazionale di Roma ("Museum" of the Thermes"); Museo Torlonia; Musei Vaticani: exceptional collections of ancient Roman art

– Villa Giulia; exquisite collection of Etruscan art

– Museo della Civiltà Romana; collection on cultural history erected under Mussolini in the EUR with a large model of the ancient city of Rome

Museums and Collections

Jordan

    Petra: capital of the kingdom of Nabatea, since 106 AD Roman; rock tombs with beautiful façades

Lebanon

    Baalbek: ancient Heliopolis in the Bekaa-Plain; extensive remains of temples and holy places

Libya

    Lebdah: ancient Leptis Magna; well-preserved Roman city which had been completely covered up by migrating dunes

Macedonia

    Stobi: Roman city on the Vardar with extensive late antique palace and various villas

Morocco

    Ksar Pharaoun: ancient Volubilis; well-preserved city from the time of the Roman emperors

Spain

    Madrid: Museo Arqueológico Nacional and Prado: important collection of Roman art as well as regional finds

    Mérida: Museo de Arte Romano; collection of Roman art of the region; numerous ruins of ancient Augusta Emerita in the surrounding area

    Tarragona: Museo Arqueológico; art and cultural historical collection of regional finds

Switzerland

    Augst: Roman villa and Museum; informative presentation of the finds and history of the Roman capital of the province Augusta Raurica (Kaiseraugst); impressive ruins of the city

    Avenches: ruins of ancient Aventicum with interestingly designed museum

    Brugg: Vindonissa-Museum; culture and history of of the Roman settlement Vindonissa; ruins of the settlement in nearby Windisch

    Zurich: Schweizerisches Landesmuseum; general overview of Roman settlements in today's Switzerland

Syria

    Tadmor: ancient Palmyra with well-preserved Roman buildings, among others temple of Baal

Tunisia

    Dougga: ancient Thugga; well-preserved city from the time of the Roman emperors

    El-Djem: Museé Archéologique; finds from the region, especially mosaics; important remainders of ancient Thysdrus

    Sousse: Musée Archéologique; art and cultural historical collection of regional finds

    Tunis: Musée National du Bardo; main museum for Roman finds from all over Tunisia

Turkey

    Aksu in Pamphylia; ancient Perge; numerous well-preserved buildings from Roman times

    Belkis in Pamphylia; ancient Aspendos; best-preserved Roman theater in Asia Minor

    Geyre in Caria; ancient Aphrodisias; many well-preserved buildings of the early and middle Roman empire

    Istanbul: Archaeological Museum; apart from numerous Roman antiquities from all over Turkey, informative collection on the history of the city

    Selcuk: Ephesos-Museum; overview of the excavations in Ephesos

    Selimiye in Pamphylia; ancient Side; many well-preserved buildings from Roman times

United States

Boston: Museum of Fine Arts; exquisite collection of Roman art

Malibu: J. Paul Getty Museum; one of the best collections of Roman art in this exact copy of an ancient Roman villa

New York: Metropolitan Museum of Art; art museum with numerous ancient Roman attractions

Selected Bibliography

Ackermann, J.S. *Palladio.* Harmondsworth, UK: Penguin, 1977.

Ades, D., ed. *Art and Power. Europe under the Dictators: 1930–1945.* London: Hayward Gallery, 1995.

Alföldi, A. *Early Rome and the Latins.* Ann Arbor: University of Michigan Press, 1965.

Andreae, B. *The Art of Rome.* New York: Harry N. Abrams, 1977.

Aubert, J.J. *Business Managers in Ancient Rome.* New York: E.J. Brill, 1994.

Barnes, T.D. *The New Empire of Diocletian and Constantine.* Cambridge, MA: Harvard University Press, 1982.

Barrett, J.C., ed. *Barbarians and Romans in North-West Europe.* Oxford: B.A.R., 1989.

Beachham, R.C. *The Roman Theatre and its Audience.* Cambridge, MA: Harvard University Press, 1992.

Boardman, J. *The Greeks Overseas.* Harmondsworth, UK: Penguin, 1980.

Boardman, J., J. Griffin, and O. Murray, eds. *The Oxford History of the Roman World.* Oxford: Clarendon Press, 1991.

Boyd, C.E. *Public Libraries and Literature in Ancient Rome.* Chicago: Chicago University Press, 1915.

Brilliant, R. *Roman Art from the Republic to Constantine.* London: Phaidon, 1974.

Brown, P. *The Making of Late Antiquity.* Cambridge, MA: Harvard University Press, 1978.

Burford, A. *Craftsmen in Greek and Roman Society.* London: Thames and Hudson, 1972.

Burnett, A. *Coinage in the Roman World.* London: Seaby, 1987.

Cantarella, E. *Pandora's Daughters. The Role and Status of Women in Greek and Roman Antiquity.* Baltimore: Johns Hopkins University Press, 1987.

Casson, L. *Ships and Seamanship in the Ancient World.* Princeton, NJ: Princeton University Press, 1971.

Chaitkin, W. "Roman America." *Architectural Design,* vol. 49 (1979), pp. 8–15.

Clark, J.R. *The Houses of Roman Italy.* Berkeley: University of California Press, 1991.

Coles, J. *Experimental Archaeology.* London: Academic Press, 1979.

Crawford, M. *The Roman Republic.* Cambridge, MA: Harvard University Press, 1978.

Cristofani, M. *The Etruscans: A New Investigation.* London: Orbis, 1979.

Cunliffe, B. *Rome and her Empire.* London: Constable, 1994.

Dilke, O.A.W. *Greek and Roman Maps.* Ithaca, NY:

Bibliography

Cornell University Press, 1985.

Dixon, S. *The Roman Family.* Baltimore: Johns Hopkins University Press, 1992.

Dunbabin, T.J. *The Western Greeks.* Oxford: Clarendon Press, 1968.

Duncan-Jones, R. *The Economy of the Roman Empire.* New York: Cambridge University Press, 1982.

Dupont, F. *Daily Life in Ancient Rome.* Oxford: Blackwell, 1993.

Elsner, J. *Art and the Roman Viewer: The Transformation of Art from the Pagan World to Christianity.* Cambridge: Cambridge University Press, 1995.

Exhibition Catalog. *London: The Western Greeks.* Venice/London: Thames and Hudson, 1996.

Exhibition Catalog. *London/Barcelona/Berlin: Art and Power: Europe under the Dictators 1930–1945.* London: Oktogon, Hayward Gallery, 1996.

Exhibition Catalog. *Los Angeles: Roman Portraits: Aspects of Self and Society, 1st Century BC to 3rd Century AD.* Los Angeles: Regents of the University of California, Loyola Marymount University, and the J.P. Getty Museum, 1980.

Exhibition Catalog. *Wealth of the Roman World AD 300–700.* London: British Museum Publications, 1977.

Favro, D. *The Urban Image of Augustan Rome.* New York: Cambridge University Press, 1996.

Field, G.G. *Evangelist of Race: The Germanic Vision of Houston Stewart Chamberlain.* New York: Columbia University Press, 1981.

Friedländer, L. *Roman Life and Manners under the Early Empire, 4 vol.* New York: Arno, 1928–36.

Galinsky, K. *Augustan Culture.* Princeton, NJ: Princeton University Press, 1996.

Garnsey, P. *Trade in the Ancient Economy.* Berkeley: University of California Press, 1983.

Garnsey, P., and R. Saller. *The Roman Empire: Economy, Society and Culture.* London: Duckworth, 1987.

Gjerstad, E. *Early Rome, 3 vols.* Lund, Sweden: C.W. K. Gleerup, 1953–60.

Grant, M. *The Fall of the Roman Empire.* London: Weidenfeld and Nicolson, 1976.

Greenhalgh, M. *The Classical Tradition in Art.* London: Duckworth, 1978.

Greenhalgh, M. *The Survival of Roman Antiquities in the Middle Ages.* London: Duckworth, 1989.

Guinness, D., and J.T. Sadler. *Mr. Jefferson, Architect.* New York: Viking, 1973.

Hammond, N.G.L., and H.H.S. Scullard, eds. *The Oxford Classical Dictionary.* Oxford: Clarendon Press, 1970.

Hannestad, N. *Roman Art and Imperial Policy.* Aarhus, Denmark: Aarhus University Press, 1986.

Harris, W.V. *War and Imperialism in Republican Rome.* Oxford: Clarendon Press, 1979.

Heather, P.J. *Goths and Romans.* Oxford: Clarendon Press, 1991.

Hinz, B. *Art in the Third Reich.* Oxford: Basil Blackwell, 1980.

Hitchcock, H.R., and W. Seale. *Temples of Democracy. The State Capitols of the U.S.A.* New York: Harcourt Brace Jovanovich, 1976.

Hodder, I., ed. *Archaeological Theory in Europe: The Last Three Decades.* London: Routledge, 1991.

Hodge, A.T. *Roman Aqueducts and Water Supply.* London: Duckworth, 1992.

Humphreys, J.H. *Roman Circuses.* Berkeley: University of California Press, 1986.

James, E. *The Franks.* Oxford: Blackwell, 1988.

Johnson, A. *Roman Forts of the 1st and 2nd Century AD in Britain and the German Provinces.* London: A & C Black, 1983.

Johnson, S. *Rome and Its Empire.* New York: Routledge and Keegan Paul, 1989.

Jones, A.H.M. *Studies in Roman Government and Law.* Oxford: Basil Blackwell, 1960.

Jones, A.H.M. *The Later Roman Empire 284–602.* Baltimore: Johns Hopkins University Press, 1986.

Jones, A.H.M. *The Roman Economy.* Oxford: Blackwell, 1974.

Bibliography

Knox, Bernard. *The Norton Book of Classical Literature.* New York: W.W. Norton, 1993.

Krautheimer, R. *Early Christian and Byzantine Architecture.* New Haven, CT: Yale University Press, 1980.

Le Glay, Marcel, Jean-Louis Voisin, and Yann Le Bohec. *A History of Rome.* Cambridge, MA: Blackwell, 1996.

Liberati, Anna Maria, and Fabio Bourbon. *Ancient Rome: History of a Civilization that Ruled the World.* New York: Stewart, Tabori & Chang, 1996.

Liebeschuetz, J. *Continuity and Change in Roman Religion.* Oxford: Clarendon Press, 1979.

Lintott, A. *Imperium Romanum: Politics and Administration.* London: Routledge, 1993.

Lomas, K. *Rome and the Western Greeks 350 BC–200 AD: Conquest and Acculturation in Southern Italy.* London: Routledge, 1993.

MacCormack, S.G. *Art and Ceremony in Late Antiquity.* Berkeley: University of California Press, 1981.

MacDonald, W.L. *The Architecture of the Roman Empire,* 2 vols. New Haven, CT: 1982/1986.

MacMullan, R. *Roman Social Relations 50 BC to AD 284.* New Haven, CT: Yale University Press, 1974.

Marchand, S.L. *Down from Olympus: Archaeology and Philhellenism in Germany 1750–1970.* Princeton: Princeton University Press, 1996.

Morey, C.R. *Early Christian Art.* Princeton, NJ: Princeton University Press, 1953.

Nielsen, I. *Thermae et Balnea. The Architecture and Cultural History of Roman Public Baths.* Aarhus, Denmark: Aarhus University Press, 1993.

O'Connor, C. *Roman Bridges.* Cambridge: Cambridge University Press, 1995.

Pallottino, M. *A History of Earliest Italy.* Ann Arbor: University of Michigan Press, 1991.

Parker, S.T. *Romans and Saracens. A History of the Arabian Frontier.* Philadelphia, PA: American Schools of Oriental Research, 1986.

Percival, J. *The Roman Villa.* London: Batsford, 1976.

Raaflaub, K., ed. *Between Republic and Empire. Interpretations of Augustus and his Principate.* Berkeley: University of California Press, 1990.

Reinhold, M. *Classica Americana: The Greek and Roman Heritage in the United States.* 1984.

Richardson, L. *Pompeii: An Architectural History.* Baltimore: Johns Hopkins University Press, 1988.

Ridgway, D.R., ed. *Italy before the Romans.* New York: Academic Press, 1979.

Robinson, O.F. *Ancient Rome: City Planning and Administration.* New York: Routledge, 1992.

Rodgers, W.L. *Greek and Roman Naval Warfare.* Annapolis, MD: U.S. Naval Institute, 1964.

Rodley, L. *Byzantine Art and Architecture: An Introduction.* Cambridge: Cambridge University Press, 1994.

Rostovtzeff, M. *The Social and Economic History of the Roman Empire.* Oxford: Clarendon, 1966.

Salmon, E.T. *The Making of Roman Italy.* Ithaca, NY: Cornell University Press, 1982.

Scarborough, J. *Roman Medicine.* Ithaca, NY: Cornell University Press, 1969.

Scarre, Chris. *The Penguin Historical Atlas of Ancient Rome.* London: Penguin, 1995.

Scobie, A. *Hitler's State Architecture: The Impact of Classical Antiquity.* Philadelphia: Pennsylvania State University Press, 1990.

Scobie, A. "Slums. Sanitation and Mortality in the Roman World." *Klio,* vol. 68 (1986), pp. 399–433.

Scullard, H.H. *Festivals and Ceremonies of the Roman Republic.* Ithaca, NY: Cornell University Press, 1981.

Solomon, Jon. *The Ancient World in the Cinema.* New York: 1978.

Stambaught, J.E. *The Ancient Roman City.* Baltimore: Johns Hopkins University Press, 1988.

Bibliography ... Index of Places

Starr, C.G. *The Roman Imperial Navy*. Chicago: Ares, 1993.

Stevenson, J. *The Catacombs: Rediscovered Monuments of Early Christianity*. London: Thames & Hudson, 1978.

Syme, R. *The Roman Revolution*. New York: Oxford University Press, 1967.

Torelli, M. *Typology and Structure of Roman Historical Reliefs*. Ann Arbor: University of Michigan Press, 1982.

Vanggaard, J.H. *The Flamen. A Study in the History and Sociology of Roman Religion*. Copenhagen: Museum Tusculanum Press, 1988.

Veyne, P. *Bread and Circuses*. London: Penguin, 1992.

Wacher, K., ed. *The Roman World*. London: Routledge and Keegan Paul, 1987.

Wallace-Hadrill, A. *Augustan Rome*. London: Bristol Classical, 1993.

Ward-Perkins, B. *From Classical Antiquity to the Middle Ages*. Oxford: Oxford University Press, 1984.

Webster, G. *The Roman Imperial Army of the First and Second Centuries*. London: Constable, 1996.

Weiss, R. *The Renaissance Discovery of Classical Antiquity*, 2nd edition. Oxford: Oxford University Press, 1988.

White, K.D. *Greek and Roman Technology*. Ithaca, NY: Cornell University Press, 1984.

Winkes, R. ed. *The Age of Augustus*. Providence, RI: Brown University, Center for Old World Archaeology, 1985.

Yavetz, Z. *Slaves and Slavery in Ancient Rome*. New Brunswick, NJ: Transaction Books, 1988.

Zanker, P. *The Power of Images in the Age of Augustus*. Ann Arbor: University of Michigan Press, 1988.

Index of Places

Abritus 104
Achaea 38
Actium 33, 44
Africa 37, 88, 113, 150
Aix-la-Chapelle 104, 127f
Alcantara 102
Alexandria 45
Alps 8, 90, 167
America (USA) 127, 142f, 145
Apennine 8f, 11, 13
Aquae Sextiae 25
Aquilea 158
Aquitania 88
Arabian Peninsula 88, 121
Arausio 25
Arles 119, 140, 144
Armenia 88, 90
Arnsburg 91
Aschaffenburg 91
Asia 38, 88
Asia Minor 8, 13, 37, 39, 89, 117
Aspendos 72
Assyria 88
Athens 16, 24, 38, 57ff, 63, 87, 142
Augst = Augusta Raurica 95, 114
Austria 91, 93, 99, 155
Avignon 101

Baalbek 160
Babylon 8
Bad Homburg 149
Baiae 59f, 86
Balkan 150, 159
Barletta 128
Basel 95, 114
Belgica 88
Benevent 53, 84, 170
Berlin 125, 154f
Bologna 8, 11, 126
Bonn 93
Boscoreale 55

Index of Places

Britain/Britannia 33, 88, 109
Bucharest 125
Budapest 93
Bulgaria 91, 93
Byzantium see Constantinople

Calabria 11
Cambridge 124
Campania 11f
Cannae 36
Canosa, Apulia 10
Capitoline Hill 56
Cappadocia 88, 90
Capri 54f
Capua 24
Carnuntum 154f
Carthage 8, 13, 32, 36
Castelgandolfo 56
Caulonia 8
Cerveteri 15, 16, 17, 159
Chaeronea 24
Charlottesville 124, 144f
Chaux 124
Chicago 125
Chiusi 159
Cilicia 88
Cologne (Colonia Claudia Ara Agrippinensium) 93, 95, 171
Colonia Ulpia Traiana (Xanten) 93, 95, 159
Como 125, 153
Constantinople (Byzantium) 110, 120f
Corinth 9, 37, 64
Corsica 13, 36f
Cosa 36
Crete 88
Croton 8
Cumae 8
Cyprus 88
Cyrene 88

Dacia 88f
Danube 88, 90ff, 149, 154f
Darmstadt 125
Delos 39

Delphi 36
Derbyshire 124
Deutz 95
Dura Europos 116, 120

Egypt 8, 74, 88, 106, 117, 129
Elbe 90
Elea (Velia) 8
England 91f, 102, 127, 142
Epidaurus 61
Epirus 39
Etruria 11–19, 27
Euphrat 116, 120

Fiesole 11
Forum Romanum 21, 26, 29, 44, 73, 76, 89, 104, 134, 142
France 39, 101f, 140, 142, 144f, 149
Frankfurt 91f
Fuccino, Lake 70

Gabii 65
Galatia 88
Gallia cisalpina 88
Gallia Narbonensis 88
Gaul 44, 78, 89f, 93, 99, 107
Germania (superior and inferior) 88, 90ff, 148
Germany 91, 93, 95, 100, 102, 146ff
Greece 12, 24, 30, 37, 39, 44, 57, 61, 89, 104, 116f, 120, 122, 124, 137, 147, 158, 161f
Guadiana 61

Haltern 159
Heilbronn 91
Heraclea in Siris 8
Herculaneum 47, 64, 68, 80, 85, 135, 158, 162ff
Hipponion 8
Hönningen on the Rhine 91
Hungary 93

Iberia 37
Istanbul 149
Istria 100

Jerusalem 89, 104, 123
Judea 88

Kehlheim 91, 125
Kempten 159, 169
Kos 87
Künzig 93

La Coruña 102
La Graufesenque 78
Laos 8
Las Vegas 125
Latium 56
Leontium 10
Lippe 90, 95
Locri 8
London 51f, 124f
Lorch 91
Lucca 131f
Lugdunensis 88
Lüneburg 128f
Lydian kingdom 8

Macedonia 36f, 88
Madrid 111
Main 98
Mainz 93, 98
Malibu 125
Mantua 124
Maria Hall in Carinthia 99
Marzabotto 12
Mauretania 88, 90
Medina 104
Mediterranean Sea 9, 32f, 37, 78, 84, 152
Medma 8
Merida 61
Mesopotamia 8, 88, 90
Messenia 8
Metapont 8
Milan 89, 104, 107
Moesia (superior and inferior) 88
Monte Testaccio (Rome) 99
Monticello, VA 124, 145
Moscow 125

Index of Places

Naples/Neapolis 8, 9, 32, 59, 86, 158, 162ff, 166
Naxos 10
Nea Anchialos 120
Nemi, Lake 158
Netherlands 93, 95
Neumagen 74
Neuss 86, 93
Nicaea 117
Niederwald 148
Nijmegen 93
Nîmes 19, 60, 143ff
Niniveh 8
Noreia 25
Noricum 88, 90
Northern Africa 89, 94
Numantia 37
Numidia (Africa nova) 88

Olympia 162
Orange 101, 144
Oropos 87
Orvieto 12, 16, 19
Ostia 32, 64, 66, 68, 77, 98, 151ff, 159

Padua 140
Paestum (Poseidonia) 8, 9
Palatine Hill 25f, 54, 56, 61, 159
Palestine 117
Palestrina 17
Palmyra 160
Pandosia 8
Pannonia 88
Paris 118, 124f, 129, 142ff
Pavia 126
Pergamon 37f
Persia 104
Petronell 154
Philippi 101, 117, 120
Piazza Armerina 113f
Pithekusai 8
Pompeii 22f, 47, 62, 64, 67ff, 73, 75ff, 82ff, 87, 97, 99, 100, 154, 158f, 162ff
Pontus 88, 135
Populonia 13, 18
Portici 164ff

Poseidonia see Paestum
Praeneste 48, 65
Provence 13, 101, 145
Puteoli 32
Pydna 37
Pyrgi 15f
Pyxus 8

Quirinal Hill 26, 64, 152

Raetia 88, 90
Ravenna 112, 120, 126
Regensburg 93
Remagen 93
Rhegium (Reggio/Calabria) 8f
Rhine 90ff, 95, 98, 149
Riace 58
Richmond, Virginia 124, 143, 146
Rimini 124, 139
Romania 91
Rubicon 44
Rüdesheim 148f

Saalburg 91f, 109, 149
Sahara 91, 94
Sanssouci 136
Sardinia 13, 36f, 88
Scandinavia 104
Schleswig 133
Scotland 91, 102
Scylletium 8
Sèvres 129
Sicily 9, 25, 32, 36f, 39, 58, 88, 113f
Spain 36f, 39, 61, 88, 102f, 121
Sparta 8
Sperlonga 54
Split 56, 104, 119
Stabiae 32
Sybaris 8
Syracuse 9f, 24
Syria 88

Tagus (Tejo) 102
Talamone 19
Tarentum 8, 24, 36
Tarquinia 11, 16, 159

Tarragona 103
Taunus 91f
Temesa 8
Terina 8
Teutoburg Forest 146ff
Thessalonica 89, 110, 120
Thrace 88
Tiber 32, 47, 99, 133, 152
Tiburtinum 48
Tivoli 48, 56f, 158
Trebizond 122
Trier 89, 93, 107, 110, 119, 159
Tuscany 11, 132
Tusculum 48
Tyrrhenian Sea 9

Vatican 133f, 159
Veii 11
Vesuvius, Mount 47, 68, 78, 82f, 162f, 165, 167
Vetera 93, 95, 159
Vienna 49, 52, 154
Vienne 39
Villanova 8, 11
Viminal Hill 64
Volsinii 12
Volubilis 94
Vulci 16, 18, 159

Wales 102
Walldürn 92, 100
Washington, DC 124f, 145f
Welzheim 92, 100
Westerwald 91f
Wörlitz 124

Xanten (Colonia Ulpia Traiana) 93, 95, 133, 159, 168f

Zagreb 15
Zancle (Catana) 10

Index of Names

Index of Names

Accius, Lucius (170–ca. 86 BC), poet 44

Achill(es), legendary Greek hero 23

Aemilius Paullus, Lucius (ca. 228–160 BC), politician and military leader 24

Aeneas, legendary ancestor of the Romans 20

Aerobindus (506 AD), consul 112

Aesculapius, God 21

Agricola = Gnaeus Julius Agricola (40–93 AD), military leader 167

Alberti, Leon Battista (1404–72), humanist, artist 139

Alexander the Great (*356, 336–323 BC), Macedonian king 24, 68f, 159

Alkamenes (5th century BC), Greek sculptor 57

Allroggen-Bedel, Agnes, archaeologist 164

Ambrosius (ca. 340–397), bishop of Milan 104

Ammianus Marcellinus (ca. 330–ca. 395), historian 44

Ammonios Sakkas (175–242), philosopher 44

Ancus Marcius, legendary king 25)

Antoninus Pius = Titus Aurelius Fulvus Boionius Arrius Antoninus (*86, 138–161), emperor 91f, 131, 133

Aphrodite, Greek goddess 21

Apollo, Greek and Roman god 21

Archias (8th century BC), founder of Syracuse 9

Ares, Greek god 21

Arius (ca. 280–336 AD), founder of Arianism 104

Arminius, called Hermann in the 19th/20th centuries (ca. 17 BC–ca. 21 AD), Cheruski tribal chief 146ff

Artemis, Greek goddess 21

Asklepios, Greek god 21

Astarte, Levantine goddess 15

Asterix, comic figure 157

Athanasius (ca. 295–373), bishop of Alexandria 104

Athena Parthenos, Greek goddess 21, 59

Attalos III (171–133 BC), king of Pergamon 37

Attila (*unknown, 434–453), king of the Huns 104

Augustine, Aurelius (354–430), theologian 44

Augustus = Gaius Octavianus (*63 BC, 27 BC–14 AD), emperor 22, 32f, 35, 42, 44ff, 49, 52ff, 60ff, 83, 88, 90, 93, 101, 107, 111, 125, 128, 139f, 145, 150ff, 159

Aulus Metellius 31

Aurelian = Lucius Domitius Aurelianus (*214, 270–275), emperor 104, 106

Bellona, goddess 65

Brunelleschi, Filippo (1377–1446), architect and sculptor 138

Brutus, Lucius Iunius, legendary founder of the Roman Republic and first consul 25, 28f

Caesar, Gaius Julius (100–44 BC), politician, military leader and writer 33, 44, 51, 71, 88, 90, 93, 100f, 125, 147, 151, 157

Caligula = Gaius Julius Caesar Germanicus (*12 BC, 37–41 AD), emperor 42f

Canaletto = Giovanni Antonio Canale (1697–1768), painter 96, 134

Caracalla = Marcus Aurelius Severus Antoninus, born Septimius Bassianus (*186, 211–217), emperor 43, 70, 72, 104, 106

Carinus = Marcus Aurelius Carinus (*ca. 252, 283–285), emperor 107

Cassius Dio Cocceianus (155–235), historian 44, 85

Catilina, Lucius Sergius (108–62 BC), conspirator, opponent of Cicero 25

Cato = Marcus Porcius Cato Censorius (234–149), politician and writer 25, 38, 44, 167

Catullus, Gaius Valerius (ca. 84–ca. 54 BC), poet 44

Ceius Secundus (1st century AD), duumvir in Pompeii 77

Celsus, Aulus Cornelius (ca. 25 BC–ca. 50 AD), encyclopedian 85

Ceres, goddess 21

Chamberlain, Houston Stewart (1855–1927), writer and philosopher 147

Champollion, Jean François (1790–1832), archaeologist 15

Charlemagne (*747, 768–814), Franconian king, since 800 Roman emperor 104, 123

Charles III of Bourbon (*1716, 1759–88), Spanish king = Charles IV king of Naples-Sicily (1734–59) 162

Cicero, Marcus Tullius (106–43 BC), philosopher, politician, rhetorician 25, 44, 58f

Index of Names

Cincius (ca. 210 BC), senator 25

Claudius = Tiberius Claudius Nero Germanicus (*10 BC, 41–54 AD), emperor 70, 88

Cleisthenes (6th century BC), Athenian politician 24

Cleopatra = Cleopatra VII Philopator (*69, 51–30 v. Chr.), Egyptian pharaoh 157

Cock, Hieronymus, artist 134

Columella, Lucius Iunius Moderatus (1st half of the 1st century), writer on agronomy 167

Concordia, goddess 21

Confucius (ca. 551–ca. 479), philosopher 24

Constantine I the Great = Gaius Flavius Valerius Constantinus (*ca. 280, 306–327, since 324 single ruler), emperor 53, 76, 89, 110, 117

Constantius I (*ca. 250, 293–306), emperor of the tetrarchy 51, 107, 110

Cornaro, Giorgio (16th century), Italian aristocrat 141

Crassus, Marcus Licinius (115–53 BC), politician and triumvirate 44f

Crispinus 103

Croesus (*unknown, ca. 560–546 BC), last king of Lydia 8

Cyrus II the Great (*unknown, 559–529 BC), founder of the ancient Persian empire 8

Dagobert I (*ca. 605/610, 623–639), Merowingian king 126

Dahn, Felix (1834–1912), jurist, historian, writer 149

David, Jacques Louis (1748–1825), painter 25, 137, 144

Decius = Gaius Messius Quintus Traianus Decius (*190/200, 249–251), emperor 104

Demeter, Greek goddess 21

Desgodetz, Antoine (17th century), architect and artist 160f

Diana, goddess 21

Diocletian = Gaius Aurelius Valerius Diocletianus (*ca. 245, 284–305, †313), emperor (founder of the tetrarchy) 56, 72, 89, 104, 107, 109ff, 132

Diodorus (90–ca. 20 BC), historian 44

Domitian = Titus Flavius Domitianus (*51, 81–96), emperor 43, 56, 61, 115

Dosio, Giovanni Antonio (1533–ca. 1600), artist 134

Draco (2nd half of the 7th century BC), Greek legislator 8

Eder, Walter, historian 36

Eutropius (middle of 4th century AD), historian 156

Fabius Pictor, Quintus (end of 3rd century BC), annalist 25

Fabius Rufus, house owner in Pompeii 83

Faustina, Annia Galeria (104 or 105–140 or 141), wife of Antoninus Pius 131, 133

Fehr, Burkhard, archaeologist 171

Fides, god 21

Fiorelli, Giuseppe (19th century), archaeologist 165f

Fittschen, Klaus, archaeologist 170

Flavius Josephus = Joseph ben Mathitjahu (37 or 38–after 100 AD), Jewish-Roman historian 44

Fomin, I., Russian architect 125

Fontana, Domenico (1543–1607), architect 158, 163

Fortuna, goddess 21

Fraccaro, Plinio, historian 27

Franklin, Benjamin (1706–90), politician 143

Friedländer, Ludwig, historian 64

Frontinus, Sextus Julius (1st century AD), official and writer 44, 60, 103

Galen(os) from Pergamon (129–199 AD), medic 85

Galerius = Gaius Galerius Valerius Maximianus (*ca. 250, 293–311), emperor (tetrarchy) 105, 107

Gallienus = Publius Licinius Egnatius Gallienus (*ca. 213, 253–268), emperor 104

Genialis (2nd century AD), legionary 109

Geta = Publius Septimius Geta (189–212 AD), son of Septimius Severus, brother of Caracalla 106

Gibbon, Edward (1737–94), historian 111

Gobineau, Joseph Arthur (1816–82), writer and diplomat 147

Goethe, Johann Caspar (1710–82), jurist 166

Goethe, Johann Wolfgang von (1749–1832), poet and politician 160, 165f

Goya y Lucientes, Francisco José de (1746–1828), painter 162

Gracchus, Tiberius Sempronius (162–133 BC),

Index of Names

people's tribune and reformer 25, 34

Gracchus, Gaius Sempronius (153–121 BC), people's tribune and reformer 25, 34

Hadrian = Publius Aelius Hadrianus (*76, 117–138), emperor 48, 53, 56f, 65, 91f, 121, 133, 158

Hamilton, William (1788–1856), Scottish philosopher and diplomat 158

Hannibal (247 or 246–183 BC), Carthagian military leader and politician 36f

Heemskerck, Marten van (1498–1574), painter 134

Hephaestus, Greek god 21

Hera, Greek goddess 21

Hercules, god 104, 107

Herder, Johann Gottfried von (1744–1803), writer, theologian, and philosopher 160

Hermann see Arminius

Hermes, Greek god 21

Heston, Charlton, actor 72

Hitler, Adolf (1889–1945), politician 154f

Holconius Priscus (1st century AD), duumvir in Pompeii 77

Homer(os) (8th century BC), Greek poet 21

Honos, god 21

Horace = Quintus Horatius Flaccus (65–8 BC), poet 44, 49, 60

Humboldt, Wilhelm von (1767–1835), scholar and politician 134f

Janus, Etruscan-Roman god 21

Jefferson, Thomas (*1743, 1801–09, †1826), 3rd President of the USA 142ff

Jones, Inigo (1573–1652), architect 141

Julian "Apostata" = Flavius Claudius Julianus (*331, 361–363), emperor 117

Julius II = Giuliano della Rovere (*1443, 1503–13), pope 158f

Junkelmann, Marcus, archaeologist 167

Juno, goddess 20f

Jupiter, god 20f, 49, 56, 107, 143

Justinian = Flavius Petrus Sabbatius Justinianus (*482, 527–565), emperor 111f, 117, 120f, 125f

Juvenal = Decimus Junius Juvenalis (ca. 60–ca. 140), poet 44, 65

Knobelsdorff, Georg Wenzeslaus von (1699–1753), painter and architect 136

Körner, Christian Gottfried (1756–1831), friend and publisher of Friedrich Schiller 135

Kreuz, Franz, archaeologist 155

Lactantius, Lucius Caecilius Firmianus († after 317), Latin church historian 156

Lao-tze (4th–3rd century BC), philosopher 24

Lares, household gods 20, 22, 68

Lessing, Gotthold Ephraim (1729–81), critic, poet, philosopher 159

Lothar (*941, 954–986), Western Franconian king 127f

Lucretius Fronto (1st century AD), house owner in Pompeii 83

Lysippos from Sikyon (4th century BC), Greek sculptor 57

Malatesta, Sigismondo Pandolfo (1417–68), prince of Rimini 139

Mani (ca. 216–ca. 276), Persian founder of Manicheism 104

Marcellus, Marcus Claudius (42–23 BC), nephew of Augustus 133

Marcus Aurelius = Marcus Aurelius Antoninus, born Marcus Annius Verus (*121, 161–180), emperor 53, 108, 148, 158

Marie-Antoinette von Habsburg (1755–93), French queen 136

Marius, Gaius (um 158/157–86), politician 25, 101

Mark Antony = Marcus Antonius (82–30), politician and military leader 33, 44f

Marquardt, Joachim, historian 41

Mars, god 21

Martial = Marcus Valerius Martialis (40–104), writer of epigrams 44

Maxentius = Marcus Aurelius Valerius Maxentius (*ca. 279, 306–312), emperor of the tetrarchy and opponent of Constantine 76

Maximian = Marcus Aurelius Valerius Maximianus Herculius (*ca. 250, 286–305, †310), emperor of the tetrarchy (with Diocletian) 107

Index of Names

Mercury, god 21

Michelangelo Buonarroti (1475–1564), sculptor, painter, and architect 158

Minerva, goddess 20f

Montesquieu = Charles de Secondat, Baron de la Brède et de Montesquieu (1689–1755), writer, political philosopher 142

Muhammad (570–632), founder of the Islam 104

Mussolini, Benito (1883–1945), politician 150ff

Myron from Eleutherai (ca. 480–430 BC), sculptor 57

Nashu ash-Shilahi al-Matraki 121

Nepos = Nepos Cornelius (95–30 BC), historian and biographer 44

Neptune, god 21

Nero = Lucius Domitius Ahenobarbus Nero (*37 AD, 54–68), emperor 14, 43, 55f, 64, 66, 85, 115, 157, 159f

Nerva = Marcus Cocceius Nerva (*30, 96–98), emperor 66

Numa Pompilius, legendary Roman king 25

Numerian = Marcus Aurelius Numerius Numerianus (*235, 283–284), emperor 107

Odysseus, legendary Greek hero 54

Ostrogorsky, Georg, historian 122

Otho = Marcus Salvius Otho (*32 AD, 1/30–4/16/69), emperor 128

Ovid = Publius Ovidius Naso (43 BC–17 AD), poet 44, 49

Palladio, Andrea = Andrea di Pietro (1508–80), architect and theoretician 124, 140f, 160

Pannini, Giovanni Paolo (1691–1765), painter and architect 133

Paul (ca. 10–ca. 64 AD), apostle 64

Pausanias (ca. 150–200), Greek writer 44

Penates, household gods 20

Penthesilea, legendary Greek heroine 23

Pérac, Etienne de, artist 134

Peter = Simon (†64 AD), apostle 118, 123

Phidias (5th century AD), Greek sculptor 57, 59

Piranesi, Giovanni Battista (1720–78), artist and architect 96, 117, 134ff

Plautus, Titus Maccius (?) (ca. 250–184 BC), writer of comedies 44

Pliny the Elder = Gaius Plinius Secundus (ca. 23/24–79 AD), writer, officer, official 44, 50, 58ff, 87, 159

Pliny the Younger = Gaius Plinius Caecilius Secundus (61/62–ca. 113 AD), jurist, official, author of letters 44, 47f, 54

Plutarch(os) from Chaironeia (ca. 46–ca. 120 AD), biographer 24, 38, 44

Polybius (ca. 200–120 BC), Greek historian 44

Polykletes = Polykleitos from Argos (5th century BC), Greek sculptor 57, 62

Polyphemus, legendary Greek giant 54

Pompey = Gnaeus Pompeius Magnus (106–48 BC), politician, military leader 44, 67, 76, 84

Poseidon, Greek god 21

Praxiteles (4th century BC), Greek sculptor 57

Primus (1st century AD), dyer of cloth from Pompeii 79

Proiecta (4th century AD), aristocrat 115

Remus, legendary figure 24

Roma, goddess 63

Romulus, legendary founder of Rome 24

Sallust = Gaius Sallustius Crispus (86–34 BC), politician and historian 44, 156

Schilling, Johannes (1828–1910), sculptor 148

Scipio = Publius Cornelius Scipio Africanus maior (ca. 235–183), politician and military leader 37

Seneca, Lucius Annaeus (4 BC–65 AD), politician, poet, and philosopher 14, 44, 71

Septimius Severus = Lucius Septimius Severus Pertinax (*145 or 146, 193–211), emperor 51, 66, 104, 106, 134, 142

Servius Tullius, legendary Roman king 25

Siddhartha = Buddha (ca. 560–ca. 480 BC), founder of Buddhism 24

Siegfried, figure in German legends 146

Solon (ca. 640–after 561 BC), Athenian legislator, politician, and poet 8

Spartacus (†71 BC), Thracian slave 25, 40

Speer, Albert (1905–81), politician and architect 154

Spengler, Oswald (1880–1936), philosopher 112

Index of Names

Strabo (64/63 BC – after 23 AD), Greek geographer and historian 44

Suetonius = Gaius Suetonius Tranquillus (*ca. 70 AD, †unknown), biographer 53, 55, 85

Suleiman II the Magnificent (1520–66), Osmanic sultan 121

Sulla = Lucius Cornelius Sulla Felix (138–78 BC), politician 38, 101

Tacitus, Publius Cornelius (*ca. 55/56 AD, †unknown) 44, 93, 147

Tarquinius Priscus, legendary Roman king 25

Tarquinius Superbus, legendary Roman king 25

Terentius Neo (1st century AD), citizen of Pompeii 75

Terragni, Giuseppe (1904–43), architect 153

Theoderich (*ca. 453, 471–526), Ostrogoth king 104

Theodosius I = Flavius Theodosius (*347, 379–395), emperor 43, 111, 117, 126

Thucles, Greek founder of Leontium 10

Thucydides from Athens (ca. 460–after 400 BC), Greek historian 9f

Tiberius = Tiberius Claudius Nero (*42 BC, 14–37 AD), emperor 46, 54f, 90

Timaios from Tauromaion (4th/3rd century BC), Greek historian 25

Titian = Tiziano Vecelli(o) (1477/87/90–1576), Italian painter 156

Titus = Titus Flavius Vespasianus (*39, 79–81), emperor 89, 159

Trajan = Marcus Ulpius Traianus (*53, 98–117), emperor 43, 47, 52f, 72, 84, 88f, 91, 100, 103, 151, 170

Tullius Hostilius, legendary Roman king 25

Ulpianus, Domitius (†223), jurist 114

Ustinov, Sir Peter Alexander (*1921), actor, dramatist, and director 157

Valerian = Publius Licinius Valerianus (*ca. 200, 253–260), emperor 104

Varro, Marcus Terentius (116–27 BC), writer 25

Varus, Publius Quintilius (46 BC–9 AD), military leader 90, 148

Venus, goddess 21, 51

Verres, Gaius (ca. 115–43 BC), politician 25, 58f

Vespasian = Titus Flavius Vespasianus (*9 AD, 69–79), emperor 42

Victoria, goddess 21, 50

Virgil = Publius Vergilius Maro (70–19 BC), poet 44, 49

Virtus, god 21

Vitruvius = Vitruvius Pollio (1st century BC), military technician, engeneer, and architect 18, 83, 139f, 153

Vulcan(us), god 21

Wagner, Richard (1813–83), composer 147

Wallmoden-Gimborn, Graf (1736–1811), general and diplomat 129

Wedgwood, Josiah (1730–95), potter 49

Wiegand, Theodor (1864–1936), archaeologist 149

Wilhelm II of Hohenzollern (*1859, 1888–1918, †1941), German emperor 149

Winckelmann, Johann Joachim (1717–68), archaeologist 142, 159f, 165

Zanker, Paul, archaeologist 62

Zeus, Greek God 20f

Picture Credits

Agenzia di Promozione Turistica, Lucca 190

Gottfried Aigner, Munich 66

Archiv für Kunst und Geschichte, Berlin 25, 93, 215

Archäologisches Institut der Universität Hamburg 38, 60, 61, 62, 67, 73, 80, 81, 82, 99, 102, 106, 108, 109, 125, 131, 133, 134, 135, 136, 139, 149, 154, 157, 158, 164, 165, 166, 203, 210

Bayrische Verwaltung der staatlichen Schlösser, Gärten und Seen (Photo: Maria Custodis) 195

Bayerische Staatsbibliothek, Munich 69

E. Böhm, Mainz 96, 152, 155

Bibliothèque Municipale, Autun 174

Bildarchiv Foto Marburg 41

Bildarchiv Huber, Garmisch-Partenkirchen 1

Bildarchiv Preußischer Kulturbesitz, Berlin 3, 150, 206

Brian Brake 126

C.A.T. Medienproduktion, Reichling 115, 228

Cinetext GmbH, Frankfurt 218

Collection Bertarelli, Milan 226

© 1997 Les Editions Albert René/Goscinny-Uderzo 143 (Asterix and the Satellite City), 219 (Asterix and Cleopatra)

Johannes Eue, Cologne 204

Peter Furmanek, Hannover 186

Galleria Nazionale, Parma 194

Giunti Martello Archive 5, 10, 12, 13, 17, 18

The J. Paul Getty Museum, Malibu 20, 88 (Photography provided courtesy of Bruce White), 32, 46, 47, 56

Rainer Hackenberg, Cologne 170, 178

IFA Bilderteam, Munich 70

Michael Jeiter, Morschenich 184

Kunsthistorisches Museum, Vienna 58

Landesamt für Denkmalpflege, Hesse 209

Landschaftsverband Rheinland (Archäologischer Park/Regionalmuseum Xanten und Landesbildstelle Düsseldorf) 230

Library of the Cathedral, Verona 181

Löbl-Schreyer, Bad Tölz-Ellbach 146, 185

Rolf Legler, Munich 85, 86

Sandu Mendrea, Jerusalem 180

MGM 91

Musée des Antiquités Nationales, Saint-Germain-en-Laye 44

Musée du Louvre, Paris 4, 26, 68, 197

Musei Vaticani 23, 132, 220

Museo del Prado, Madrid 217, 224

Museo Nazionale, Naples 83, 87, 97

Museum of Art, Rhode Island School of Design, Mary B. Jackson Fund, Providence, RI 95

National Gallery of Art, Washington DC 175

Ny Carlsberg Glyptotek, Copenhagen 48, 49

PubliAerFoto, Milan 7

Roger-Viollet, Paris 202

© Albert Speer Archiv, Heidelberg 216

Saalburgmuseum, Bad Homburg 156

Lambert Schneider, Hamburg 78, 79, 229

Soprintendenza Archeologica di Roma 027

Staatliche Münzsammlung, Munich 39

Staatsgalerie, Stuttgart 188

Süddeutscher Verlag, Munich 207

E. Thiem, Lotos Film, Kaufbeuren 21, 22, 24, 29, 30, 34, 37, 45, 52, 53, 54, 57, 59, 63, 71, 75, 77, 84, 89, 100, 101, 103, 107, 117,118, 137, 145, 151, 160

Martin Thomas, Aix-la-Chapelle 74, 191, 199

University library, Istanbul 176

Virginia Museum, Richmond 50

Yale University Art Gallery, New Haven 168

Fulvio Zanettini, Cologne 64, 65, 121, 179, 189, 213

Camilla Zimmermanns, Pullach 201

Günter Zwingelberg, Kirchlinteln 205

The illustration nr. 90 we took from the book Was ist Was, vol. 82, Gladiatoren, with the friendly permission of Tessloff-Verlag, Nuremberg

Maps and charts: DuMont Buchverlag, Cologne

All rights for illustrations not mentioned here belong to the author, the publisher, or could not be located.